YOUR F

YOUR  NAME

OR,

KABALISTIC ASTROLOGY

BEING THE HEBRAIC METHOD OF DIVINATION
BY THE POWER OF SOUND, NUMBER,
AND PLANETARY INFLUENCE

BY

"SEPHARIAL"

Author of "The Manual of Astrology," "A Manual
of Occultism," "The Kabala of Numbers,"
"Second Sight," etc

THIRD EDITION

NEWCASTLE PUBLISHING CO. INC.
NORTH HOLLYWOOD, CALIFORNIA
1981

A NEWCASTLE BOOK
FIRST PRINTING OCTOBER 1981
PRINTED IN THE UNITED STATES OF AMERICA

PREFACE TO THE THIRD EDITION

THE remarkable success which has attended the publication of this work through two editions renders it convenient to issue a further edition, and I take this opportunity of drawing attention to one or two points raised in the course of correspondence with my readers.

The Twenty-two Major Points of the Tarot are, as explained further in my " Manual of Occultism," nothing less than hieroglyphical keys to the stages of Initiation. They represent the Ten, Seven and Three steps of the Three Degrees of attainment ; and they culminate in points XXI. and XXII., that is to say, in the Crown of the Magi or The Fool. The significance of the perfect numbers 10, 7 and 3 in the stages of Initiation are well marked by X., The Sphinx; XVII., The Star of the Magi; and XX., The Awakening of the Dead. They represent (a) the conquest of the four elements of the natural world—scientific attainment ; (b) the conquest of the sidereal world by a knowledge of cosmic science ; (c) the conquest of the spiritual world. These three points or keys remain in their original places in the scheme of the Tarot. Some others have been rearranged.

The science of Numbers—Numerology—has recently attracted a great deal of attention in Occult circles. Several important clues to interpretation will be found in these pages.

Attention must be given to the question whether the horoscope is diurnal or nocturnal, as if it be diurnal or a " morning " horoscope, the Sun's position must be taken from the calendar for the preceding date. The application of this principle to some of the examples given in these pages may reveal apparent errors of calculation, but it may be borne in mind that I have in most cases availed myself of the astronomical facts, and have held but indifferently to the Theban Calendar, which, while presenting some anomalies, is deemed sufficiently simple to be of service to those uninstructed in the use of an ephemeris.

I take this opportunity of correcting some views of my horoscopes of Cecil Rhodes, and others, whose full names are not employed in the calculations of their respective key numbers. Since it appears that a change of name involves a change of fortune, the substitution of a husband's name for a lady's maiden name reveals by Kabalism the nature of the change thus effected in the life and fortunes.   Similarly, the addition of a name to the baptismal name of a man will int oduce new elements into the destiny ; and the obscuration of a name, although baptismal, will effect, or be indicative of, a corresponding elimination of certain elements from the career of a person.

Cecil John Rhodes was potentially Jack Rhodes, John Rhodes, Cis Rhodes, or Cecil Rhodes.   The fact that he graduated as plain Cecil, charges that name with the full import of the destiny.   It is similarly the case with regard to the baptismal names of Royalty, many of which are traditional, others complimentary, and one only—that which is the ordinary appellative—of any material significance.

While expressing my appreciation of the many cases submitted to me for solution by the Kabalistic method, I regret that the calls made upon my time do not permit of the individual attention I should like to give them, and I trust, therefore, that these remarks will clear the ground of some difficulties to which my correspondents have referred, and enable them to complete their studies without further trouble.

SEPHARIAL.

PREFACE TO THE SECOND EDITION

IN the preparation of the following work I am indebted to the writings of the French Kabalist and Astrologer, Eliphas Levi, to those of Mons. P. Christian, and the popular work upon the Horoscope by M. Ely Star, who, in conjunction with other Continental Astrologers, has popularized the more extensive and deep researches of the Kabalists, bringing their conclusions into a more or less systematic form.   The object of the present Manual is the presentation of this system, which has already attained some standing on the Continent, to English-reading Astrologers.

The present revised and enlarged edition of the work will be found to contain examples of the use of Kabalism in connection with Political Astrology, this being an entirely new application of the Power of Numbers and an extension of the Kabalistic System which I feel sure will be of interest to students.   New examples have been added to those already published, and the work in its present form will, I trust, meet with the approval of those interested in this phase of occultism

SEPHARIAL.

CONTENTS

CHAP		PAGE
I	THE REQUIRED DATA	11
II	THE CYCLIC TABLE OF YEARS	13
III	THE NUMBER OF A NAME	15
IV	THE SEVEN PLANETARY CIRCLES	17
V	POINTS OF DEPARTURE	26
VI	HOW TO ERECT THE HOROSCOPE	28
VII	THE TWELVE HOUSES AND SIGNS	32
VIII	THE PLANETS	35
IX	GENERAL RULES	37
X	LUNAR POINTS	39
XI	JUDGMENT BY POSITION	42
XII	PLANETS IN THE TWELVE SIGNS	43
XIII	JUDGMENT FROM THE THIRTY-ONE POINTS	54
XIV	DITTO DECANS	56
XV	ANNUAL REVOLUTIONS	58
XVI	THE EIGHTH CIRCLE	67
XVII	GENERAL EXAMPLES No. I	72
XVIII	DITTO No. II	77
XIX	DITTO No. III	79
	DITTO No. IV	82
	DITTO No. V	84
	DITTO No. VI	86
XX	POLITICAL HOROSCOPES	88
XXI	THE TAROT	91

INTRODUCTION

A SYSTEM of Astrology which is based entirely upon the power of names and numbers, considered Kabalistically, is apparently quite strange to English-reading students of the Astral Science. It is with some confidence, therefore, that I pen a work of this kind to commence a series of Astrological Manuals, believing as I do that every sincere truth-seeker is prepared to recognize whatever of truth there may be in any speculation that has engaged the minds of mystical researchers, or added to the sum of possible knowledge.

Kabalistic Astrology is based, as I have said, upon the power of Names and Numbers. Essentially all names are numbers, and all numbers are names; that is to say, the one is resolvable into the other. Thus it is said in the Apocalypse: Here is wisdom. Let him that hath understanding count the number of the beast, for it is the number (name) of a man; and his number is *Six hundred three-score and six.*

A name is a mantram, an invocation, a spell, a charm. It gains its efficacy from the fact that in pronunciation certain vibrations, corresponding to the mass-chord of the name, are set up; not only in the atmosphere, but also in the more ethereal substance, referred to by a modern philosopher as " mind stuff," whose modifications form the basis for changes of thought. This is evident to us in the fact that names, when sounded, import to our minds certain characteristics, more or less definite according to the acuteness of our psychometric sense. How different, for instance, are the impressions conveyed to us in the names, " Percy " and " Horatio " in " George " and " Ralph," in " Eva " and " Ruth." Seeing, then, what different characteristics are conveyed to us in these and other names, it will not seem wholly improbable that a difference of fortune and destiny should go along with them. In Scripture we have evidence of the name carrying with it a peculiar destiny and of the naming of persons and things according to their dominant characteristics, as is in the case of Eve (*Hevah*) " the mother " ; Jacob, " the supplanter " ; Ishmael, " the striver," etc. ; and in the naming of the brute creation the animals were brought before Adam to see what he would call them, " and whatsoever he called them, that was the *name* thereof." Likewise, when Leah brought forth a son, she said, " Gad ariseth," and she called the name of him Gad, i.e., Jupiter, the planet being then on the horizon. Gad means " a horseman," and Jupiter is the lord of Sagittarius. The modern name Walter has a similar signification, and belongs like Percy to the sign Sagittarius. A change of name is accompanied by a change of destiny, as in the case of Abram and Abraham, of Jacob and Israel. Whoever, therefore, shall take the name of a family, takes also the destiny attaching thereto, and this may happen by inheritance or by marriage.

But the Kabala affords proof of its canons, and in the system of Astrology which is based upon the numerical value of names we have one of the many examples of practical proof which the " Science of Numbers " affords. As the learned astronomer, Camille Flammarion, says : If the mysteries of the Kabala have no objective reality, they may yet have a reality in the subjective world. It is the fact that the numerical basis of Kabalism has a significance in the world of causes that makes it possible of demonstration in the world of effects, where all number becomes form and sound, and takes on an objective reality, following the order and nature of their subjective antecedents. It is undoubtedly a rational concept, and was so esteemed among the Gnostics with whom the *Verbum* or *Logos* (the Word) was the Creative Energy. So in the Gnostic fragment preceding the Gospel of John, it is said : In the beginning was the Word. . . . All things were made by Him, and without Him was not anything made which was made. By the Kabalists the word *Deber* was the creative power of the *Alhim*, the sevenfold male-female Potency of primeval order.

The well-known French mystic, M. P. Christian, says in regard to the name conferred upon individuals at the time of the first ceremony or initiation : At the hour of birth something has already had place in the life of the child, it is the Name which completes the generation. When our soul creates or evokes a thought, the image of that thought engraves itself in the Astral Fluid, which is the receptacle and mirror of all manifestations of being.

The image expresses the *thing*, the *thing* is the virtue or soul of the symbol. To utter a word is to evoke a thought and to render it present : the magnetic power of the human speech is the beginning of all manifestation in the occult world. To confer a *name*, is not only to define a being, but also to devote it, by the emission of the *Verbum*, to the influence of one or several occult forces. Things are, for each of us, that which we make them in the *naming*. The *Verbum*, or the Word of each man is, although unknown to him, a benediction or a curse ; that is why ignorance of the properties of the *idea* and of *matter* is to us so often direful.

Yes, names are benefic or malefic ; they are, in a sense, poisonful or healthful, according to the hidden influences that the Supreme Wisdom attaches to their elements, that is to say, to the *letters* which compose them, and to their correlates in *numbers*.

Number, says Balzac, is to our Spirit as it is to matter, an incomprehensible agent. Is it a Being, is it a breath emaned from God for the organizing of the material Universe—where nothing takes its form save by the Divinity—which is an effect of Number ? Are not the least as the greatest of created things distinguished from one another by their quantities, qualities, dimensions, and forces, all the attributes engendered by Number ? The infinity of numbers is a fact proved to your mind, but of which no proof whatever can be given materially. The mathematician will tell us that the infinite in numbers exists, but does not pourtray itself : God is a number possessed of motion, and cognises, but does not reveal himself. As the Unity, he is the beginning of numbers, with which he has nothing in common. The existence of Number depends upon Unity, which, itself without number, engenders them all. God is the great Unity, who has nothing in common with his creations, and who, nevertheless, produces them. But, what ! you, who can neither measure the first Abstraction that God has revealed to you, nor grasp it, would yet investigate the Secret Sciences that proceed from Deity ? What would it avail, then, did I plunge you in the abysms of Motion, the force that disposes Number ?   What would it matter did I add that both Motion and Number are engendered by the Word, the Supreme Reason of the Seers and the Prophets, who, in ancient times, heard the mighty breathing of the Deity, as the Apocalypse testifies ?

Let it suffice if we show, in the present work, that the Astrologer can raise, howsoever little, the corner of the great veil which hides the mysteries of the future from the eyes of men.   We shall prove the power of Name and of Number ; we shall open up some of the mysteries of the four elements and their mother, the Great Athanor of the Mages.   Of the fruitful Earth, inexhaustible mother of the human species, as of " great beasts and creeping things " ; of the Ocean, mother of the Continents and of the Leviathan, and hosts of creatures as yet unknown to us ; of the Sacred Element of Fire, creator, transmuter, and destroyer, symbol of the Triune Deity, whose form is incognizable ; of the Air, which is the vehicle of our energy and life, whose coming and going is an alternating birth and death to the myriad " lives " which swarm within our physical structure ; of the Ether—force, light, motion, heat in one—which interpenetrates the molecular spaces of the densest bodies, under-lying all substances, perhaps itself substantial yet beyond our sense-perception, the Astral Fluid and the Mother-Substance of sublunary things : of these we shall inquire concerning the destiny of man, which hitherto has been hidden from us in mysterious symbol, in sound, in form, in number and in name.   Let us proceed !

KABALISTIC ASTROLOGY

CHAPTER I.

THE REQUIRED DATA.

1. *The Christian and Surname.*

It has been already stated in the Introduction that the name is the basis of the horoscope framed according to the rules of the Kabala. In this the Surname stands for, and is significant of, the fate or destiny attaching to the family whose members hold that name in common. The Christian or fore-name, or names, are those which distinguish the personality of the Native from the common type of the family. Just as there is a family likeness in point of feature between the several members of one family, and just as any one member may be distinguished by a certain individuality due to feature, form, stature, and manner of bearing ; so the family name is a type in Sound and Number of a certain destiny attaching to that family, while the several Christian or personal names of the members thereof give to each a distinctive fate which proceeds from the specialized attributes of the Ego inhering in the body of each, and expressed in the name. For the purpose of erecting the Kabalistic Horoscope, it is therefore necessary to set down the full Christian and Surname of the Native.

2. *Morning or Evening Birth.*

In Astrology the day begins at noon, and from the noon till midnight is called " evening," while from midnight till the following noon is called " morning." Thus in Scripture it is said, " And the evening and the morning were the first day " ; clearly indicating that the Kabalistic record was in harmony with astronomical and astrological canons. If, therefore, a person be born at 6 p.m., the horoscope is called an " evening " one. But on the other hand, if the birth have place at 6 a.m., it is a " morning " horoscope.

Now observe, the " morning " horoscope belongs to the *preceding* noon, and this is important, as the place of the sun has to be taken at that time according to the calendar which is hereafter set forth.

N.B.—In the case of persons born on the 1st January in any year, if between midnight and noon, the last day of the old year preceding must be taken as that of birth ; because, as was said, the " morning " horoscope belongs to the preceding noon. The *year* of birth will be thus altered.

3. *The Sun's Longitude.*

The following are the longitudes of the Sun upon the several days of the year, as determined by the Kabalistic Calendar. There being 366 days in the year, and 360° in the Zodiacal Circle, some days carry the same degree, and these will be noted as they occur. By noting the degree which enters with the first day of each month, the degree corresponding to any other day in the month may be known by simple calculation.

THE CALENDAR.

January 1st   —   11° Capricorn.
February 1st   —   12° Aquarius.
    N.B.—There are 29 days in this month.
March 1st   =   11° Pisces.
April 1st   =   12° Aries.
May 1st   =   12° Taurus.
    N.B.—The 20th and 21st of this month both take the 1st degree of Gemini, and the 30th of the month takes the 10th degree of Gemini, as also does the 31st of the month.
June 1st   =   11° Gemini.
    N.B.—The 21st and 22nd of June both take the 1st degree of Cancer.
July 1st   =   10° Cancer.
    N.B.—The 22nd and 23rd of July both take the 1st degree of Leo, and the 30th and 31st of the month take the 8th degree of Leo.
August 1st   =   9° Leo.
    N.B.—The 30th and 31st of August take the 8th degree of Virgo.
September 1st =   9° Virgo.
October 1st   =   9° Libra.
November 1st =   10° Scorpio.
December 1st =   10° Sagittarius.

4. *The Moon's Age.*

This is necessary to be known, as many of the calculations from the horoscope are made in respect to the Moon's position ; for example the length of life and the kind of death, which is judged from the Moon's position, counted from Aries or Libra, according as the Moon is coming from the New to the Full, or the reverse ; which calculations will be explained in their appropriate place.

A rule for finding the Moon's age at any period will be found in Chapter X under the heading of "Lunar Points," but the information is also contained in most of the popular almanacs, and one of these for the required year will serve. As old almanacs are difficult to obtain, however, a general rule has been given which will render the student independent of this source of information.

CHAPTER II

The Cyclic Table of Years

The circle of years is divided into periods of 36 years each, which periods are successively ruled over by the planets Saturn, Jupiter, Mars, etc., in a certain order, viz.: in the reverse order of the days of the week. Each period is again subdivided by the rulership of the planets in the natural and Kabalistic order, viz.: Saturn, Jupiter, Mars, Sun, Venus, Mercury, and the Moon. It is this subdivision which becomes of importance in the calculation of the horoscope, for the planet ruling over it determines the Circle of Fortune which is to be regarded in any particular case. The 36-year Cycles are as follows:—

Saturn opens and closes the years A.D. 1 to 36 inclusive, 253 to 288, 506 to 540, 757 to 792, 1009 to 1044, 1261 to 1296, 1513 to 1548, 1765 to 1800.

Venus opens and closes the years A.D. 37 to 72 inclusive, 289 to 324, 541 to 576, 793 to 828, 1045 to 1080, 1297 to 1332, 1549 to 1584, 1801 to 1836.

Jupiter opens and closes the years A.D. 73 to 108 inclusive, 325 to 360, 577 to 612, 829 to 864, 1081 to 1116, 1333 to 1368, 1585 to 1620, 1837 to 1872.

Mercury opens and closes the years A.D. 109 to 144 inclusive, 361 to 396, 613 to 648, 865 to 900, 1117 to 1152, 1369 to 1404, 1621 to 1656, 1873 to 1908.

Mars opens and closes the years A.D. 145 to 180 inclusive, 397 to 432, 649 to 684, 901 to 936, 1153 to 1188, 1405 to 1440, 1657 to 1692, 1909 to 1944.

Moon opens and closes the years A.D. 181 to 216 inclusive, 433 to 468, 685 to 720, 937, 972, 1189 to 1224, 1441 to 1476, 1693 to 1728, 1945 to 1980.

Sun opens and closes the years A.D. 217 to 252 inclusive, 469 to 504, 721 to 756, 973 to 1008, 1225 to 1260, 1477 to 1512, 1729 to 1764, 1981 to 2016.

The above series may be extended to cover any years previous to the Christian Era, or subsequent to the year 2016, but for all practical purposes the period covered will serve, as showing the principle of the cyclic dominion of the planets.

It will be seen that the reign of Queen Victoria began with one of the cycles of Jupiter, a most happy augury! The present year is under the dominion of Mercury, which continues to rule till 1908. Under its influence it may be expected that Science and Literature will make rapid strides, together with means of international communication, travelling accommodation, dietetic reforms and sanitation hygiene, etc., in short all things ruled by the 3rd and 6th Houses and under the general influence of Mercury. But to return.

For the purpose of erecting horoscopes, and for the more ready determination of the planet presiding over any year, the Cycles and Sub-cycles from 1765 to 1908 A.D., are here set out in their order. The planet ruling the Sub-cycle, or *year of birth*, is the one to be remarked for practical purposes, as will hereafter be shown.

CYCLE OF SATURN.

Saturn	..	..	..	1765	1772	1779	1786	1793	1800.
Jupiter	..	..	..	1766	1773	1780	1787	1794
Mars	..	..	..	1767	1774	1781	1788	1795
Sun	..	..	..	1768	1775	1782	1789	1796
Venus	..	..	..	1769	1776	1783	1790	1797
Mercury	..	..	..	1770	1777	1784	1791	1798
Moon	..	..	..	1771	1778	1785	1792	1799

CYCLE OF VENUS.

Venus	..	..	..	1801	1808	1815	1822	1829	1836.
Mercury	..	..	..	1802	1809	1816	1823	1830
Moon	..	..	..	1803	1810	1817	1824	1831
Saturn	..	..	..	1804	1811	1818	1825	1832
Jupiter	..	..	..	1805	1812	1819	1826	1833
Mars	..	..	..	1806	1813	1820	1827	1834
Sun	..	..	..	1807	1814	1821	1828	1835

CYCLE OF JUPITER.

Jupiter	..	..	..	1837	1844	1851	1858	1865	1872.
Mars	..	..	..	1838	1845	1852	1859	1866
Sun	..	..	..	1839	1846	1853	1860	1867
Venus	..	..	..	1840	1847	1854	1861	1868
Mercury	..	..	..	1841	1848	1855	1862	1869
Moon	..	..	..	1842	1849	1856	1863	1870
Saturn	..	..	..	1843	1850	1857	1864	1871

CYCLE OF MERCURY.

Mercury	..	..	..	1873	1880	1887	1894	1901	1908.
Moon	..	..	..	1874	1881	1888	1895	1902
Saturn	..	..	..	1875	1882	1889	1896	1903
Jupiter	..	..	..	1876	1883	1890	1897	1904
Mars	..	..	..	1877	1884	1891	1898	1905
Sun	..	..	..	1878	1885	1892	1899	1906
Venus	..	..	..	1879	1886	1893	1900	1907

It is credibly affirmed that the great French astrologer and physician, Michael Nostradamus, made use of the Cyclic Law of planetary influence in the construction of his famous quatrains. The student will find the edition by Garencières to contain many conspicuous examples of this great Kabalist's prophetic power. That mysterious satellite of Napoleon Buonaparte, L'homme Rouge des Tuileries, is reported by P. Christian to have made use of the present system of Kabalism for the guidance of his patron, whose downfall was primarily due to the inordinate ambition which caused the Emperor to continue his campaign after the astrologer had declared the zenith of fame to have been reached. The name of L'homme Rouge was Pierre Leclerc.

CHAPTER III

The Number of a Name.

As every Name is the equivalent of a certain Number, so each letter which composes the Name has its own numerical value. These values are not arbitrary, but are those which have been used by the Rosicrucians and Kabalists from the earliest times, and are apparently derived from the Hebrew Alphabet. The following table shows the corresponding values of the English Alphabet, the assignment of the values of the letters being a matter which has fully satisfied numerous tests, so as to leave it in no doubt whatever.

A = 1 ; B = 2 ; C = 2 ; D = 4 ; E = 5 ; F = 8 ; G = 3 ; H = 8
I = 1 ; J = 1 ; K = 2 ; L = 3 ; M = 4 ; N = 5 ; O = 7 ; P = 8
Q = 1 ; R = 2 ; S = 3 ; T = 4 ; U = 6 ; V = 6 ; W = 6 ; X = 6
Y = 1 ; Z = 7.

It is now necessary to show the use that is made of this Numerical Alphabet in the computation of a name for Astrological purposes.

To this end it is needful to choose an example, and I therefore set down the name of the Ex-Premier of England,

William Ewart Gladstone

This name must be written vertically, each of the components making a separate column. The values of the several letters in each of the names are set against them according to the above Alphabet, and the multiples from 1 onwards must be set against them in order, so that the first letter in each name may be multiplied by the number of the total of letters in the name ; the second letter by one less, and so on ; the last letter in each name being set down in its own units value. Thus :—

W = 6 × 7 = 42	E = 5 × 5 = 25	G = 3 × 9 = 27
I = 1 × 6 = 6	W = 6 × 4 = 24	L = 3 × 8 = 24
L = 3 × 5 = 15	A = 1 × 3 = 3	A = 1 × 7 = 7
L = 3 × 4 = 12	R = 2 × 2 = 4	D = 4 × 6 = 24
I = 1 × 3 = 3	T = 4 × 1 = 4	S = 3 × 5 = 15
A = 1 × 2 = 2		T = 4 × 4 = 16
M = 4 × 1 = 4		O = 7 × 3 = 21
		N = 5 × 2 = 10
		E = 5 × 1 = 5
Total 84	Total 60	Total 149

The Statesman was born in the year 1809, on the 29th December. As the Statesman was born in the morning of that day, the nativity must be referred to the previous noon, viz. : the 28th December.

To recapitulate our work so far as we have gone, let us collect the data for this nativity.

It will be seen from the previous chapter that the year 1809 is in the Cycle of Venus, and falls under the influence of Mercury. This latter is therefore the ruling planet of the year.

The Sun's position must next be considered. The 28th December —which we said was the Astrological date of birth, instead of the 29th, as in the ordinary Calendar which counts from midnight to midnight—gives for the Sun's longitude Capricorn 7°. This will be found at the end of Chapter I, where the Sun's place for 1st December is given as 10° Sagittarius. If we add 1 degree for each succeeding day, on the 28th December—27 days afterwards—we shall have 7° Capricornus, i.e., the 7th degree of the 10th sign of the Zodiac.

It is now necessary to collect the numbers derived from the names: William, 84; Ewart, 60; and Gladstone, 149; together with the above position of the Sun 7° of the 10th sign, and extend them thus :—
8460149710 .. 40, in the year or circle of Mercury.
We are now ready to go a stage further in our elucidations.

The question may arise as to whether the parental name or that of the husband should be used as surname in the case of a married woman. To this I reply most assuredly the parental name should be used. By means of it the destiny regarding marriage, so frequently the subject of inquiry, may be extracted from the horoscope. Marriage is an event already included in the horoscopes of those who are destined to marry, and is therefore a result of the congenital disposition of the stars. Our studies, in fact, will show that the birth and naming of a child may not be, apparently is not, a matter of chance at all, but that birth, name, and environment are as much a result of planetary influence as are the fortunes subsequently experienced as the result of inherent character working through a definite environment and heredity.

In all cases, therefore, the surname of the father must be taken into the calculation, whether for male or female horoscopes. What happens after the marriage of a girl is largely dependent on the horoscope of the husband, which should be considered.

CHAPTER IV

THE SEVEN PLANETARY CIRCLES

THE Planetary Circles, which are extended in the following pages, are otherwise known as the " Circles of Fate." The arrangement of them, which in itself appears the more marvellous the more they are studied, dates back to the highest antiquity. The modern well-known occultist, Eliphas Levi, adopted them in his work upon the Hermetic Tarot, which he called the " Bible of Humanity."

Each Circle consists of 78 Arcana, of which the first 22 are called Greater Arcana, and the remaining 56 are called Lesser Arcana. The Greater Arcana, or, as I shall hereafter call them, " *Points,*" are the same for each Circle ; the remaining 56 Points vary according to the Planetary Circle which may be taken. For horoscopical purposes it must be understood that the following Tables are in reality *Circles,* as they are indeed called ; and each of the seven circles uniformly commences at the same Point, proceeds through the 22 Major Points, and passes by 56 Lesser Points which are peculiar to each of the Circles, and so round again to the First Major Point.

The Point at which entry is to be made into the Circle of the year of birth, which must be under one of the Seven Planets, is determined by the Decan held by the Sun at the time of birth. But this will need separate consideration.

The Seven Planetary Circles here follow on in their order :—

MAJOR POINTS OF THE SEVEN CIRCLES.

No.	Point.	Planet.	Sign
1	i.		
2	ii.	D	
3	iii.	♀	
4	iv.	♃	
5	v.	♂	♈
6	vi.	D	♉
7	vii.	☉	♊
8	viii.	♀	♋
9	ix.	♃	♌
10	x.	☿	♍
20	xi.	♂	
30	xii.	D	♎
40	xiii.		
50	xiv.	☉	♏
60	xv.	♄	♐
70	xvi.	♃	♑
80	xvii.	☿	
90	xviii.	♀	♒
100	xix.	♃	♓
200	xx.	♄	
300	xxi.	☉	
400	xxii.		

CIRCLE OF SATURN.

The XXII. Major Points, then:

9	..	..	xxiii.	..	..Royal Star..	..	♌
5	..	..	xxiv.	..	♄	..	♈
6	..	..	xxv.	..	♀	..	♉
7	..	..	xxvi.	..	♃	..	♊
1	..	..	xxvii.	..	Sceptre	..	..
2	..	..	xxviii.	..	☽	..	..
3	..	..	xxix.	..	♀	..	..
4	..	..	xxx.	..	♃	..	..
5	..	..	xxxi.	..	♃	..	♈
6	..	..	xxxii.	..	☿	..	♉
7	..	..	xxxiii.	..	☽	..	♊
8	..	..	xxxiv.	..	♂	..	♋
9	..	..	xxxv.	..	☽	..	♌
10	..	..	xxxvi.	..	☉	..	♍
6	..	..	xxxvii.	..	..Royal Star..	..	♉
8	..	..	xxxviii.	..	☉	..	♋
9	..	..	xxxix.	..	♄	..	♌
10	..	..	xl.	..	♃	..	♍
20–1	..	..	xli.	..	♂	..	..
30–2	..	..	xlii.	..	♀	..	♎
40–3	..	..	xliii.	..	Reaper	..	..
50–4	..	..	xliv.	..	♃	..	♏
60–5	..	..	xlv.	..	☿	..	♐
70–6	..	..	xlvi.	..	☽	..	♑
80–7	..	..	xlvii.	..	☿	..	..
90–8	..	..	xlviii.	..	☉	..	♒
100–9	..	..	xlix.	..	♄	..	♓
200–10	..	..	l.	..	♄	..	..
90	..	..	li.	..	..Royal Star..	..	♒
30	..	..	lii.	..	☿	..	♎
50	..	..	liii.	..	♂	..	♏
60	..	..	liv.	..	☉	..	♐
1	..	..	lv.	..	Sword	..	..
2	..	..	lvi.	..	☽	..	..
3	..	..	lvii.	..	♀	..	..
4	..	..	lviii.	..	♃	..	..
5	..	..	lix.	..	♂	..	♈
6	..	..	lx.	..	☉	..	♉
7	..	..	lxi.	..	♄	..	♊
8	..	..	lxii.	..	♀	..	♋
9	..	..	lxiii.	..	☿	..	♌
10	..	..	lxiv.	..	♂	..	♍
50	..	..	lxv.	..	..Royal Star..	..	♏
70	..	..	lxvi.	..	♄	..	♑
90	..	..	lxvii.	..	♀	..	♒
100	..	..	lxviii.	..	☿	..	♓
20–1	..	..	lxix.	..	♂ Crowned ..		
30–2	..	..	lxx.	..	☽	..	♎
40–3	..	..	lxxi.	..	Reaper	..	..
50–4	..	..	lxxii.	..	♄	..	♏
60–5	..	..	lxxiii.	..	♀	..	♐
70–6	..	..	lxxiv.	..	♃	..	♑
80–7	..	..	lxxv.	..	☿	..	..
90–8	..	..	lxxvi.	..	♂	..	♒
100–9	..	..	lxxvii.	..	☽	..	♓
200–10	..	..	lxxviii.	..	♄	..	..

CIRCLE OF JUPITER.

The **XXII**. Major Points, then:

9	xxiii.	Royal Star	♌
5	xxiv.	♃	♈
6	xxv.	☿	♉
7	xxvi.	♂	♊
1	xxvii.	Sceptre	..
2	xxviii.	☽	..
3	xxix.	♀	..
4	xxx.	♃	..
5	xxxi.	♂	♈
6	xxxii.	☽	♉
7	xxxiii.	♄	♊
8	xxxiv.	☉	♋
9	xxxv.	♄	♌
10	xxxvi.	♀	♍
6	xxxvii.	Royal Star	♉
8	xxxviii.	♀	♋
9	xxxix.	♃	♌
10	xl.	♂	♍
20–1	xli.	♂	..
30–2	xlii.	☿	♎
40–3	xliii.	Reaper	..
50–4	xliv.	♂	♏
60–5	xlv.	☽	♐
70–6	xlvi.	♄	♑
80–7	xlvii.	☿	..
90–8	xlviii.	♀	♒
100–9	xlix.	♃	♓
200–10	l.	♄	..
90	li.	Royal Star	♒
30	lii.	☽	♎
50	liii.	☉	♏
60	liv.	♀	♐
1	lv.	Sword	..
2	lvi.	☽	..
3	lvii.	♀	..
4	lviii.	♃	..
5	lix.	☉	♈
6	lx.	♀	♉
7	lxi.	♃	♊
8	lxii.	☿	♋
9	lxiii.	☽	♌
10	lxiv.	☉	♍
50	lxv.	Royal Star	♏
70	lxvi.	♃	♑
90	lxvii.	☿	♒
100	lxviii.	☽	♓
20–1	lxix.	♂ Crowned	..
30–2	lxx.	♄	♎
40–3	lxxi.	Reaper	..
50–4	lxxii.	♃	♏
60–5	lxxiii.	☿	♐
70–6	lxxiv.	♂	♑
80–7	lxxv.	☿	..
90–8	lxxvi.	☉	♒
100–9	lxxvii.	♄	♓
200–10	lxxviii.	♄	..

CIRCLE OF MARS.

The XXII. Major Points, then:

9	..	..	..	xxiii.	..	..Royal Star..		..	♌
5	..	..	..	xxiv.	..	.. ♂	..	..	♈
6	..	..	..	xxv.	..	.. ☽	..	..	♉
7	..	..	..	xxvi.	..	.. ☉	..	..	♊
1	..	..	..	xxvii.	..	.. Sceptre	..	..	..
2	..	..	..	xxviii.	..	.. ☽	..	..	..
3	..	..	..	xxix.	..	.. ♀	..	..	..
4	..	..	..	xxx.	..	.. ♃	..	..	..
5	..	..	..	xxxi.	..	.. ☉	..	..	♈
6	..	..	..	xxxii.	..	.. ♄	..	..	♉
7	..	..	..	xxxiii.	..	.. ♃	..	..	♊
8	..	..	..	xxxiv.	..	.. ♀	..	..	♋
9	..	..	..	xxxv.	..	.. ♃	..	..	♌
10	..	..	..	xxxvi.	..	.. ☿	..	..	♍
6	..	..	..	xxxvii.	..	..Royal Star..		..	♉
8	..	..	..	xxxviii.	..	.. ☿	..	..	♋
9	..	..	..	xxxix.	..	.. ♂	..	..	♌
10	..	..	..	xl.	..	.. ☉	..	..	♍
20–1	..	..	..	xli.	..	.. ♂	..	..	..
30–2	..	..	..	xlii.	..	.. ☽	..	..	♎
40–3	..	..	..	xliii.	..	.. Reaper	..	..	..
50–4	..	..	..	xliv.	..	.. ☉	..	..	♏
60–5	..	..	..	xlv.	..	.. ♄	..	..	♐
70–6	..	..	..	xlvi.	..	.. ♃	..	..	♑
80–7	..	..	..	xlvii.	..	.. ☿	..	..	..
90–8	..	..	..	xlviii.	..	.. ☿	..	..	♒
100–9	..	..	..	xlix.	..	.. ♂	..	..	♓
200–10	..	..	..	l.	..	.. ♄	..	..	..
90	..	..	..	li.	..	..Royal Star..		..	♒
30	..	..	..	lii.	..	.. ♄	..	..	♎
50	..	..	..	liii.	..	.. ♀	..	..	♏
60	..	..	..	liv.	..	.. ☿	..	..	♐
1	..	..	..	lv.	..	.. Sword	..	..	..
2	..	..	..	lvi.	..	.. ☽	..	..	..
3	..	..	..	lvii.	..	.. ♀	..	..	..
4	..	..	..	lviii.	..	.. ♃	..	..	..
5	..	..	..	lix.	..	.. ♀	..	..	♈
6	..	..	..	lx.	..	.. ☿	..	..	♉
7	..	..	..	lxi.	..	.. ♂	..	..	♊
8	..	..	..	lxii.	..	.. ☽	..	..	♋
9	..	..	..	lxiii.	..	.. ♄	..	..	♌
10	..	..	..	lxiv.	..	.. ♀	..	..	♍
50	..	..	..	lxv.	..	..Royal Star..		..	♏
70	..	..	..	lxvi.	..	.. ♂	..	..	♑
90	..	..	..	lxvii.	..	.. ☽	..	..	♒
100	..	..	..	lxviii.	..	.. ♄	..	..	♓
20–1	..	..	..	lxix.	..	.. ♂ Crowned ..		..	..
30–2	..	..	..	lxx.	..	.. ♃	..	..	♎
40–3	..	..	..	lxxi.	..	.. Reaper	..	..	..
50–4	..	..	..	lxxii.	..	.. ♂	..	..	♏
60–5	..	..	..	lxxiii.	..	.. ☽	..	..	♐
70–6	..	..	..	lxxiv.	..	.. ☉	..	..	♑
80–7	..	..	..	lxxv.	..	.. ☿	..	..	..
90–8	..	..	..	lxxvi.	..	.. ♀	..	..	♒
100–9	..	..	..	lxxvii.	..	.. ♃	..	..	♓
200–10	..	..	..	lxxviii.	..	.. ♄	..	..	..

CIRCLE OF THE SUN.

The XXII. Major Points, then:

9	..	..	..	xxiii.	..	..Royal Star..		..	♌
5	..	..	..	xxiv.	..	.. ☉	..	..	♈
6	..	..	..	xxv.	..	.. ♄	..	..	♉
7	..	..	..	xxvi.	..	.. ♀	..	..	♊
1	..	..	..	xxvii.	..	.. Sceptre	..	..	..
2	..	..	..	xxviii.	..	.. ☽	..	..	..
3	..	..	..	xxix.	..	.. ♀	..	..	..
4	..	..	..	xxx.	..	.. ♃	..	..	..
5	..	..	..	xxxi.	..	.. ♀	..	..	♈
6	..	..	..	xxxii.	..	.. ♃	..	..	♉
7	..	..	..	xxxiii.	..	.. ♂	..	..	♊
8	..	..	..	xxxiv.	..	.. ☿	..	..	♋
9	..	..	..	xxxv.	..	.. ♂	..	..	♌
10	..	..	..	xxxvi.	..	.. ☽	..	..	♍
6	..	..	..	xxxvii.	..	..Royal Star..		..	♉
8	..	..	..	xxxviii.	..	.. ☽	..	..	♋
9	..	..	..	xxxix.	..	.. ☉	..	..	♌
10	..	..	..	xl.	..	.. ♀	..	..	♍
20–1	..	..	..	xli.	..	.. ♂	..	..	..
30–2	..	..	..	xlii.	..	.. ♄	..	..	♎
40–3	..	..	..	xliii.	..	.. Reaper	..	..	..
50–4	..	..	..	xliv.	..	.. ♀	..	..	♏
60–5	..	..	..	xlv.	..	.. ♃	..	..	♐
70–6	..	..	..	xlvi.	..	.. ♂	..	..	♑
80–7	..	..	..	xlvii.	..	.. ☿	..	..	
90–8	..	..	..	xlviii.	..	.. ☽	..	..	♒
100–9	..	..	..	xlix.	..	.. ☉	..	..	♓
200–10	..	..	..	l.	..	.. ♄	..	..	..
90	..	..	..	li.	..	..Royal Star..		..	♒
30	..	..	..	lii.	..	.. ♃	..	..	♎
50	..	..	..	liii.	..	.. ☿	..	..	♏
60	..	..	..	liv.	..	.. ☽	..	..	♐
1	..	..	..	lv.	..	.. Sword	..	..	..
2	..	..	..	lvi.	..	.. ☽	..	..	..
3	..	..	..	lvii.	..	.. ♀	..	..	..
4	..	..	..	lviii.	..	.. ♃	..	..	..
5	..	..	..	lix.	..	.. ☿	..	..	♈
6	..	..	..	lx.	..	.. ☽	..	..	♉
7	..	..	..	lxi.	..	.. ☉	..	..	♊
8	..	..	..	lxii.	..	.. ♄	..	..	♋
9	..	..	..	lxiii.	..	.. ♃	..	..	♌
10	..	..	..	lxiv.	..	.. ☿	..	..	♍
50	..	..	..	lxv.	..	..Royal Star..		..	♏
70	..	..	..	lxvi.	..	.. ☉	..	..	♑
90	..	..	..	lxvii.	..	.. ♄	..	..	♒
100	..	..	..	lxviii.	..	.. ♃	..	..	♓
20–1	..	..	..	lxix.	..	..♂ Crowned..		..	..
30–2	..	..	..	lxx.	..	.. ♂	..	..	♎
40–3	..	..	..	lxxi.	..	.. Reaper	..	..	..
50–4	..	..	..	lxxii.	..	.. ☉	..	..	♏
60–5	..	..	..	lxxiii.	..	.. ♄	..	..	♐
70–6	..	..	..	lxxiv.	..	.. ♀	..	..	♑
80–7	..	..	..	lxxv.	..	.. ☿	..	..	..
90–8	..	..	..	lxxvi.	..	.. ☿	..	..	♒
100–9	..	..	..	lxxvii.	..	.. ♂	..	..	♓
200–10	..	..	..	lxxviii.	..	.. ♄	..	..	..

CIRCLE OF VENUS.

The XXII. Major Points, then:

9	..	..	..	xxiii.	..	..Royal Star..		..	♌
5	..	..	..	xxiv.	..	.. ♀	..	..	♈
6	..	..	..	xxv.	..	.. ♃	..	..	♉
7	..	.:	..	xxvi.	..	.. ☿	..	..	♊
1	..	..	..	xxvii.	..	.. Sceptre	..	..	..
2	..	..	..	xxviii.	..	.. ☽	..	..	..
3	..	..	..	xxix.	..	.. ♀	..	..	..
4	..	..	..	xxx.	..	.. ♃	..	..	..
5	..	..	..	xxxi.	..	.. ☿	..	..	♈
6	..	..	..	xxxii.	..	.. ♂	..	..	♉
7	..	..	..	xxxiii.	..	.. ☉	..	..	♊
8	..	..	..	xxxiv.	..	.. ☽	..	..	♋
9	..	..	..	xxxv.	..	.. ☉	..	..	♌
10	..	..	..	xxxvi.	..	.. ♄	..	..	♍
6	..	..	..	xxxvii.	..	..Royal Star..		..	♉
8	..	..	..	xxxviii.	..	.. ♄	..	..	♋
9	..	..	..	xxxix.	..	.. ♀	..	..	♌
10	..	..	..	xl.	..	.. ☿	..	..	♍
20–1	..	..	..	xli.	..	.. ♂	..	..	..
30–2	..	..	..	xlii.	..	.. ♃	..	..	♎
40–3	..	..	..	xliii.	..	.. Reaper	..	..	..
50–4	..	..	..	xliv.	..	.. ☿	..	..	♏
60–5	..	..	..	xlv.	..	.. ♂	..	..	♐
70–6	..	..	..	xlvi.	..	.. ☉	..	..	♑
80–7	..	..	..	xlvii.	..	.. ☿	..	..	..
90–8	..	..	..	xlviii.	..	.. ♄	..	..	♒
100–9	..	..	..	xlix.	..	.. ♀	..	..	♓
200–10	..	..	..	l.	..	.. ♄	..	..	..
90	..	..	..	li.	..	..Royal Star..		..	♒
30	..	..	..	lii.	..	.. ♂	..	..	♎
50	..	..	..	liii.	..	.. ☽	..	..	♏
60	..	..	..	liv.	..	.. ♄	..	..	♐
1	..	..	..	lv.	..	.. Sword	..	..	..
2	..	..	..	lvi.	..	.. ☽	..	..	..
3	..	..	..	lvii.	..	.. ♀	..	..	..
4	..	..	..	lviii.	..	.. ♃	..	..	..
5	..	..	..	lix.	..	.. ☽	..	..	♈
6	..	..	..	lx.	..	.. ♄	..	..	♉
7	..	..	..	lxi.	..	.. ♀	..	..	♊
8	..	..	..	lxii.	..	.. ♃	..	..	♋
9	..	..	..	lxiii.	..	.. ♂	..	..	♌
10	..	..	..	lxiv.	..	.. ☽	..	..	♍
50	..	..	..	lxv.	..	..Royal Star..		..	♏
70	..	..	..	lxvi.	..	.. ♀	..	..	♑
90	..	..	..	lxvii.	..	.. ♃	..	..	♒
100	..	..	..	lxviii.	..	.. ♂	..	..	♓
20–1	..	..	..	lxix.	..	.. ♂ Crowned	..	..	..
30–2	..	..	..	lxx.	..	.. ☉	..	..	♎
40–3	..	..	.	lxxi.	..	.. Reaper	..	..	..
50–4	..	..	..	lxxii.	..	.. ♀	..	..	♏
60–5	..	..	..	lxxiii.	..	.. ♃	..	..	♐
70·6	..	..	..	lxxiv.	..	.. ☿	..	..	♑
80·7	..	..	..	lxxv.	..	.. ☿	..	..	..
90–8	..	..	..	lxxvi.	..	.. ☽	..	..	♒
100–9	..	..	..	lxxvii.	..	.. ☉	..	..	♓
200–10	..	..	..	lxxviii.	..	.. ♄	..	..	..

Circle of Mercury.

The XXII. Major Points, then:

9	xxiii.	Royal Star	♌
5	xxiv.	☿	♈
6	xxv.	♂	♉
7	xxvi.	☽	♊
1	xxvii.	Sceptre	..
2	xxviii.	☽	..
3	xxix.	♀	..
4	xxx.	♃	..
5	xxxi.	☽	♈
6	xxxii.	☉	♉
7	xxxiii.	♀	♊
8	xxxiv.	♄	♋
9	xxxv.	♀	♌
10	xxxvi.	♃	♍
6	xxxvii.	Royal Star	♉
8	xxxviii.	♃	♋
9	xxxix.	☿	♌
10	xl.	☽	♍
20–1	xli.	♂	..
30–2	xlii.	♂	♎
40–3	xliii.	Reaper	..
50–4	xliv.	☽	♏
60–5	xlv.	☉	♐
70–6	xlvi.	♀	♑
80–7	xlvii.	☿	..
90–8	xlviii.	♃	♒
100–9	xlix.	☿	♓
200–10	l.	♄	..
90	li.	Royal Star	♒
30	lii.	☉	♎
50	liii.	♄	♏
60	liv.	♃	♐
1	lv.	Sword	..
2	lvi.	☽	..
3	lvii.	♀	..
4	lviii.	♃	..
5	lix.	♄	♈
6	lx.	♃	♉
7	lxi.	☿	♊
8	lxii.	♂	♋
9	lxiii.	☉	♌
10	lxiv.	♄	♍
50	lxv.	Royal Star	♏
70	lxvi.	☿	♑
90	lxvii.	♂	♒
100	lxviii.	☉	♓
20–1	lxix.	♂ Crowned	..
30–2	lxx.	♀	♎
40–3	lxxi.	Reaper	..
50–4	lxxii.	☿	♏
60–5	lxxiii.	♂	♐
70–6	lxxiv.	☽	♑
80–7	lxxv.	☿	..
90–8	lxxvi.	♄	♒
100–9	lxxvii.	♀	♓
200–10	lxxviii.	♄	–

CIRCLE OF THE MOON.

The XXII. Major Points, then:

9	..	..	..	xxiii.	..	Royal Star	..	..	♌
5	..	..	..	xxiv.	..	☽	..	..	♈
6	..	..	..	xxv.	..	☉	..	..	♉
7	..	..	..	xxvi.	..	♄	..	..	♊
1	..	..	..	xxvii.	..	Sceptre	..	..	..
2	..	..	..	xxviii.	..	☽	..	..	..
3	..	..	..	xxix.	..	♀	..	..	..
4	..	..	..	xxx.	..	♃	..	..	..
5	..	..	..	xxxi.	..	♄	..	..	♈
6	..	..	..	xxxii.	..	♀	..	..	♉
7	..	..	..	xxxiii.	..	☿	..	..	♊
8	..	..	..	xxxiv.	..	♃	..	..	♋
9	..	..	..	xxxv.	..	☿	..	..	♌
10	..	..	..	xxxvi.	..	♂	..	..	♍
6	..	..	..	xxxvii.	..	Royal Star	..	..	♉
8	..	..	..	xxxviii.	..	♂	..	..	♋
9	..	..	..	xxxix.	..	☽	..	..	♌
10	..	..	..	xl.	..	♄	..	..	♍
20—1	..	..	..	xli.	..	♂	..	..	..
30—2	..	..	..	xlii.	..	☉	..	..	♎
40—3	..	..	..	xliii.	..	Reaper	..	..	..
50—4	..	..	..	xliv.	..	♄	..	..	♏
60—5	..	..	..	xlv.	..	♀	..	..	♐
70—6	..	..	..	xlvi.	..	☿	..	..	♑
80—7	..	..	..	xlvii.	..	☿	..	..	..
90—8	..	..	..	ĸlviii.	..	♂	..	..	♒
100—9	..	..	..	xlix.	..	☽	..	..	♓
200—10	..	..	..	l.	..	♄	..	..	..
90	..	..	..	li.	..	Royal Star	..	..	♒
30	..	..	..	lii.	..	♀	..	..	♎
50	..	..	..	liii.	..	♃	..	..	♏
60	..	..	..	liv.	..	♂	..	..	♐
1	..	..	..	lv.	..	Sword	..	..	..
2	..	..	..	lvi.	..	☽	..	..	..
3	..	..	.,	lvii.	..	♀	..	..	..
4	..	..	..	lviii.	..	♃	..	..	..
5	..	..	..	lix.	..	♃	..	..	♈
6	..	.•	..	lx.	..	♂	..	..	♉
7	.,	..	..	lxi.	..	☽	..	..	♊
8	..	..	..	lxii.	..	☉	..	..	♋
9	..	..	..	lxiii.	..	♀	..	..	♌
10	..	..	..	lxiv.	..	♃	..	..	♍
50	..	..	..	lxv.	..	Royal Star	..	..	♏
70	..	..	..	lxvi.	..	☽	..	..	♑
90	..	..	..	lxvii.	..	☉	..	..	♒
100	..	..	..	lxviii.	..	♀	..	..	♓
20—1	..	..	..	lxix.	..	♂ Crowned	..	..	..
30—2	..	..	..	lxx.	..	☿	..	..	♎
40—3	..	..	..	lxxi.	..	Reaper	..	..	..
50—4	..	..	..	lxxii.	..	☽	..	..	♏
60—5	..	..	..	lxxiii.	..	☉	..	..	♐
70—6	..	..	..	lxxiv.	..	♄	..	..	♑
80—7	..	..	..	lxxv.	..	☿	..	..	..
90—8	.	..	..	lxxvi.	..	♃	..	..	♒
100—9	..	.•	..	lxxvii.	..	☿	..	..	♓
200—10	..	..	..	lxxviii.	..	.	♄	..	..

By reference to the end of Chapter III it will be seen that the *Key Number* of Gladstone's horoscope is determined to be 40, in the Circle of Mercury. If reference be now made to the 50th Point in the Circle of Mercury, it will be seen that the planet Saturn is set off against that point. This will have a bearing upon the interpretation of the horoscope, when the figure is erected and judgment comes to be made of it according to the rules of the Kabalistic Art of Astrology.

CHAPTER V

POINTS OF DEPARTURE

IT is now necessary to indicate what is meant by the "Point of Departure," whereby entry is made into the circle of the year of birth. The Point, therefore, may be known by the use of the following table, and is determined entirely by the place of the Sun at birth ; as, if it were in the 1st Decan of Aries, then entry would be made at Point XXXVI in the Circle of the year of birth ; or, if in the 3rd Decan of Leo, then entry must be made at Point XL of the Circle ; and in each case this Point is known as the "Point of Departure." Thus in the case of Mr. Gladstone, the Sun being in the 1st Decan of Capricorn, entry is made into the Circle of Mercury—that being the ruler of the year 1809—at the Lth Point. The utility of carefully computing this Point, upon which the whole horoscope depends, appears to have made it convenient to frame all the 36 Points of Departure in a single Table, which is here given :—

TABLE OF POINTS OF DEPARTURE.

ARIES	.. .. ..	1st	Decan starts from	.. ..	xxxvi.
		2nd	ditto	.. ..	xxxvi.
		3rd	ditto	.. ..	LXIV.
TAURUS	.. .. ..	1st	ditto	.. ..	LXIV.
		2nd	ditto	.. ..	XXXVI.
		3rd	ditto	.. ..	XXXVI.
GEMINI	.. .. ..	1st	ditto	.. ..	XXXVI.
		2nd	ditto	.. ..	LXIV.
		3rd	ditto	.. ..	XXXVI.
CANCER	.. .. ..	1st	ditto	.. ..	XXXVI.
		2nd	ditto	.. ..	XL.
		3rd	ditto	.. ..	LXIV.
LEO	.. .. ..	1st	ditto	.. ..	LXIV.
		2nd	ditto	.. ..	XXXVI.
		3rd	ditto	.. ..	XL.
VIRGO	.. .. ..	1st	ditto	.. ..	XL.
		2nd	ditto	.. ..	LXIV.
		3rd	ditto	.. ..	XXXVI.
LIBRA	.. .. ..	1st	ditto	.. ..	L.
		2nd	ditto	.. ..	LXIV.
		3rd	ditto	.. ..	LXXVIII.
SCORPIO	.. .. ..	1st	ditto	.. ..	LXXVIII.
		2nd	ditto	.. ..	L.
		3rd	ditto	.. ..	LXIV.
SAGITTARIUS	.. ..	1st	ditto	.. ..	LXIV.
		2nd	ditto	.. ..	LXXVIII.
		3rd	ditto	.. ..	L.
CAPRICORN	.. ..	1st	ditto	.. ..	L.
		2nd	ditto	.. ..	LXXVIII.
		3rd	ditto	.. ..	LXXVIII.

AQUARIUS	..	..	..	1st	Decan starts from	..	..	LXXVIII.
				2nd	ditto	..	..	L.
				3rd	ditto	..	..	LXXVIII.
PISCES	..	..	..	1st	ditto	..	..	LXXVIII.
				2nd	ditto	..	..	LXXVIII.
				3rd	ditto	..	..	L.

It will be observed that the Points of Departure are limited to 5 in number, which taken with the 12 signs of the Zodiac, affords 60 different positions at the outset of any horoscopical figure. These Points of Departure are taken in regard to the present cycle of 1000 years, and must change after the year 1999 A.D. The reason for this will appear in the next chapter, when the construction of the horoscope is more fully developed. The principle of the distribution of these 5 Points of Departure throughout the 36 Decans will also appear upon a more careful examination of the elements which enter into the figure of the nativity. At present it is only necessary to indicate the Point due to each Decan.

CHAPTER VI

How to Erect the Horoscope

WE have now before us all the preliminary material for the purpose of erecting the horoscope. It is needful only to remind the reader that the Kabalistic system—unlike the Astronomical process usually employed, and no doubt already familiar to the intelligent student—regards the Sign held by the Sun at the time of birth as that under which a person is " born " as the saying is. In point of fact, a person is born under *all* the Signs, since each of them contributes something to the conformation of body and character, as well as fortune and destiny. But the present system, which is purely symbolical, employs the Sun's position as a central fact in nature, around which the fabric of the horoscope is fashioned, as from the *nucleolus* in the nebulous matter of abysmal space, a world obtains form and substance, and evolves in course of time to the proportions and condition of a habitable sphere. The Kabala, employing, as it does, the type of Kosmos in the world of thought, which is the world of Causation, is able to hold the destinies of all things within its mysterious veil, as all species are held in a type, as all effects are embodied in a Cause. But to proceed with the present exposition of the practical art.

Having all the data which, so to say, embody the personality of the native, viz.: the family name, the Christian names, the date of birth, the month and year (care being taken to fix the date according as the birth is " morning " or " evening," as already set forth in a previous chapter), it is now necessary to complete the *Scale of the Nativity*. This is done in the following manner. Example: William Ewart Gladstone, born December 29th, 1809 (morning nativity). We rectified the date according to rule to December 28th. We already have the Key Number of the Nativity, thus :—

$$84—60—149—7—10 \quad .. \quad 40 \text{ Mercury.}$$

The rising sign is that held by the Sun in all cases. In this instance it is Capricorn.

To the Year of Birth	..	..	1809	
Add the Key-Number		..	40	
Sum of Horoscope	..	..	1849	= X.
Surname	.. ..	..	.. 149	= XI.
Christian Names in Reverse Order {			60	= XII.
			84	= I.
Degree	..	.. ..	7	= II.
Sign	..	.. ..	10	= III.
Year	..	.. ..	1809	= IV.

The order shown here is to be followed invariably. Sometimes it will happen that a native has more than two Christian names, in which case they are set down in their reverse order as above, and each name is given to one of the Houses indicated by the Roman figures. It is not necessary that the Scale of the Nativity should cease at the 4th House as in the present instance.

To continue : the figures 1849, called the " Sum of the Horoscope," are those which, referred to the circle of Mercury ruling the year 1809, give the positions of the Planets in regard to the 10th House of the Horoscope. The surname gives the figures 149, which, on the same Circle of Mercury, are referred to the 11th House. The same may be said of the Numbers, which, in the above " Scale," are referred to the 12th, 1st, and other Houses.

The distribution of these numbers is a matter of importance, for it will be seen that the Circles of the Planets do not contain Nos. like 18 or 49, and it is therefore necessary to resolve the " Sum " 1849 into its proper constituents. This is done as follows :—

    1,000 becomes 10
     800   ,,   8
      40 remains 40
       9   ,,   9

Similarly, the Surname 149 gives: 100—40—9 ; the Christian names, 60 = 60 ; 84 = 80—4 ; the year 1809 = 10—8—9.

It will be seen that the Tables do not give any number over 400, and it therefore becomes necessary to decompose or dissect any number over that quantity.

Now, taking a figure of the heavens with the signs of the Zodiac equally disposed through the 12 Houses—the *rising sign* being always that which holds the Sun at the time of birth—on the one hand the reader may place the Circle of Mercury, and on the other the Scale of the Nativity upon a piece of paper.

The Point of Departure in the present instance, due to the Sun being in the 1st Decan of Capricorn, was determined to be 50. Referring to this in the Roman figures we find Saturn, which is placed against the 10 in the Scale. The next number in the Scale is 8, and search must be made down the column of Arabic figures for the first 8 from the Point of Departure. It is found against Point LXII. " Mars in Cancer." This is set down on the Scale opposite the figure 8. The next number in the Scale is 40, and continuing down the Column in the " Circle of Mercury " it is found at Point LXXI. " Reaper," and the symbol ♃ must be set down in the Scale opposite 40. The next figure is 9, and this is found in the Circle at Point LXXVII. " Venus in Pisces." This completes the figures due to the 10th House.

Note.—Where two numbers are given in the " Circle " against any " Point," it means that either may be taken according to requirement. Care must be taken not to miss any required number, for that would invalidate the whole of the Scale.

Proceeding now with the 11th House ; the number 149 ... 100—40 —9. The 10th House ceased at Point LXXVII., and for the figures 100 we have to pass to the beginning of the Circle, and in the 22 Major Points we find at Point XIX., opposite to 100, " Jupiter in Pisces." This is set down in the Scale opposite the No. 100. The next number, 40, is found in the Circle at Point XLIII., " Reaper," and 9, the last

number, is found to follow at Point XLIX., "Mercury in Pisces."
These complete the figures due to the 11th House.

In the same way the 12th, 1st, and other Houses in the Scale are
taken out from the Circle of Mercury, and the Scale is complete, when
it is represented as follows :—

SCALE OF THE NATIVITY.

1849 10th House	{	10 8 40 9	Saturn. Mars in Cancer. Reaper. Venus in Pisces.
149 11th House	{	100 40 9	Jupiter in Pisces. Reaper. Mercury in Pisces.
60 12th House	{	60	Jupiter in Sagittarius.
84 1st House	{	80 4	Mercury. Jupiter.
7 2nd House	{	7	Sun in Gemini.
10 3rd House	{	10	Mercury in Virgo.
1809 4th House.	{	10 8 9	Jupiter in Virgo. Jupiter in Cancer. Mercury in Leo.

The question will now arise, "How, if Libra be on the 10th House,
and Capricorn rising, can 'Mars in Cancer' be placed in the 10th
House where it is due ?" To this the answer is made, that Mars being
in Cancer must be indicated by symbol in the horoscope as being so
placed bodily, but a line drawn from it to the 10th House signifies
that a ray from that body to the 10th affects the things ruled over
by that House. The same may be said of " Jupiter in Pisces " affecting
the 11th House, and of other similar positions. This will appear more
evident when the figure of Horoscope is drawn out, when by carefully
comparing it with the " Scale " of the Nativity, it will be found that
all the requirements of the scheme are fulfilled (see Horoscope).

This horoscope is left to the intelligent reader to interpret according to the rules which will hereafter be given. The indications of
the statesman and orator are : Saturn, Lord of the figure, in its elevation in the 10th, with a ray from Venus into Libra—its own sign
—from the sign of its exaltation. Mercury and Jupiter rising in
Capricorn ; Venus, Jupiter, and Mercury conjoined in the 3rd House,
in the sign of Venus and the exaltation of Jupiter. The passing re-
verses in the career of the Statesman are seen in the presence of the
" Reaper " in the 10th, and some false allies, by its presence in the
11th ; but with Jupiter and Mercury also there, a modification, at
once subtile and beneficial, is shown, The end of life, denoted by
the 4th House, with Aries receiving the rays of Jupiter from Virgo
and Cancer, and Mercury in Leo, is fraught with some physical dangers,
serious illness, but success.

In the horoscope (p. 31) it is seen that all the Houses receive the
rays of some one or more planets, or have some planet posited therein,

with the exception of the 5th House. In this case the planet Venus, which rules the sign Taurus, is understood to be therein, and unaffected by the other planets, hence pure and unalloyed, a good augury wherever found. It is now necessary to indicate the rules by which a Nativity can be judged upon the lines of the Kabala. This will employ the succeeding chapters.

CHAPTER VII

THE TWELVE HOUSES AND SIGNS

THE presages of life are, in Astrology, resolved into twelve groups, corresponding to the 12 Houses of the Zodiac, from the affections of which in any particular horoscope judgment is drawn concerning the life and fortunes of the native. The significance of the Houses is as follows :—

The 1st House governs the disposition, aptitudes, temperament, and physical condition of the native.

2nd.—Probable fortune, gain or loss, and everything that touches the financial condition.

3rd.—That which concerns the brothers and sisters, short journeys, correspondence and means of communication.

4th.—The father, secrets of the family, changes in the position, patrimony, and landed property.

5th.—Associations of life, employments, love affairs, children, pleasures.

6th.—Strifes, discord, ill-health, family affairs, voluntary faults, servants, subjects to the native, dress, food.

7th.—Marriage, contracts, partnerships, open enemies or opponents.

8th.—Unexpected benefits, legacy, gifts, blows, wounds, cause of death, co-workers.

9th.—Misfortunes of brothers or sisters, relatives by marriage, mysteries of destiny, providential assistance, mental tastes, religion, long voyages.

10th.—Future destiny, honours, supremacy, elevation, social position, dignities, profession.

11th.—Friends, protectors, hopes and disappointments, useful relations, help from friends or the reverse.

12th.—Disagreeable things, persecutions, treasons, secret enmities, calumnies, jealousies, restraint, exile or imprisonment, captivity, sorcery.

It will, of course, be understood that the sign Aries has affinity with the First House, Taurus with the Second House, and so on. The 1st House will therefore rule the *head*, that part of the body governed by Aries. The 2nd House will rule the throat, eustachian tubes, ears, bronchial tubes, and the organs of speech and hearing generally. The 3rd House, like the Sign Gemini, will rule the arms, hands, shoulders, bones, and lungs ; and so for the other houses, each taking its rulership from the known distribution of the 12 Signs of the Zodiac over the body of man.

The distribution of the signs according to their elemental and constitutional natures is as follows :—

ELEMENTAL NATURES.

FIRE—Aries, Leo, Sagittarius.
AIR—Gemini, Libra, Aquarius.
WATER—Cancer, Scorpio, Pisces.
EARTH—Taurus, Virgo, Capricorn.

CONSTITUTIONAL NATURES.

MOVABLE—Aries, Cancer, Libra, Capricorn.
FIXED—Taurus, Leo, Scorpio, Aquarius.
COMMON—Gemini, Virgo, Sagittarius, Pisces.

Every odd sign, Aries, Gemini, etc., is masculine ; every even sign, Taurus, Cancer, etc., is feminine.

The benefic signs are : Taurus, Cancer, Leo, Virgo, Sagittarius, and Pisces.

The malefics are : Aries, Gemini, Libra, Scorpio, Capricorn, and Aquarius.

Of these, however, all are not equally good and bad alike.

The following significations of the Twelve Signs when rising in the Kabalistic horoscope will be of use to the student in the interpretation of the figure.

ARIES.—Great ambitions ; honours ; audacity ; aptitude ; courage ; fortune ; prominence.

It renders the native fickle, generous, courageous, worthy, ingenious, and well-informed.

TAURUS.—Changes ; voyages ; durable, and lasting affairs ; fruitfulness ; public affairs.

It makes the native amorous, imaginative, impulsive, laborious, calm, and patient in work ; proud.

GEMINI.—Indifferent fortunes ; accidents in the life ; inventions ; discoveries ; physical sciences and researches.

It makes the native philosophical, artistic, quick in intellect, subtile, eloquent, industrious, and of good nature.

CANCER.—Voyages by sea ; marine traffic ; life by the sea ; publicity ; good fortune ; happiness ; supremacy.

It inclines to inconstancy, dreaminess, eccentricity, prudence, good friendship.

LEO.—Great honours ; enterprises ; elevation ; glory ; celebrity.

It gives a tendency to great undertakings, ambition, constancy, nobility, kindness, generous spirit, more artistic and adventurous than learned and thoughtful.

VIRGO.—Opposition from others ; ill-fortune ; troubles in love affairs, or tardiness therein ; likewise in friendships and the marriage state ; troubles of the heart ; difficulty in attaining honours.

It renders the native wise, learned, inclined to literature, spiritual, benevolent, a lover of the occult.

LIBRA.—Unforeseen misfortunes and sorrows ; difficulty in acquiring honours ; few enemies ; some catastrophes or accidents in the life ; trouble through women.

It makes one amorous but unfaithful, sweet-tempered, just, poor, of no great literary or artistic ability.

SCORPIO.—Troubles in love ; long voyages ; dangerous wounds ;

evil tendencies, **bad counsel** ; unjust violence ; danger of drowning ; secret crimes.

It renders the native bold, warlike, quarrelsome, sarcastic, punctilious, wilful, of troublesome fancy, and false views.

SAGITTARIUS.—Success ; fortune ; chance of elevation ; strife ; distaste for the exact sciences ; mystical.

It makes the native good-tempered, kind, and obliging, flexible, a good friend, philosopher, liberal and just, loving prowess and glory.

CAPRICORN.—Unexpected sorrows ; perils ; sickness ; many envious enemies ; small chance of fortune ; love of travelling ; contests.

It makes the native wilful, stubborn, bellicose, ponderous, taciturn, economical, capricious, and liable to sudden changes of intentions and policy.

AQUARIUS.—Sorrows ; fortune ; small honours ; (in the case of a female—delay in child-birth) ; trouble through relatives ; faithful friends ; helpful protectors.

It makes the native chaste, humane, kind, inclined to solitude, righteous, just, patient in work.

PISCES.—Good fortune ; some strange troubles ; sometimes honours and elevation ; popularity ; uncertain alliances ; insecure relations.

It makes the native eloquent, spiritual, of prompt and quick mind, good understanding, difficult to know, gay, changeful, and very passionate.

The *fruitful* Signs are Taurus, Cancer, Scorpio, Sagittarius, and Pisces. *Sterile* Signs, Aries, Gemini, Leo, and Virgo.

N.B.—A more complete analysis of the properties of the Twelve Signs will be found in Sepharial's " New Manual of Astrology." In the Kabalistic system the ruling sign being that held by the Sun in the Zodiac, at the time of birth, the interpretations given above are to be applied to that sign in each horoscope ; though it will be evident that they may be applied, often times, to the sign which is *actually rising* in the orient of any particular horoscope.

CHAPTER VIII

The Planets

The *benefics* are Jupiter, the Sun, and Venus. The *malefics* are Saturn and Mars. The *neutral* planets are Mercury and the Moon. Jupiter, Venus, and the Moon, are fruitful; Saturn and Mars sterile; and Mercury is judged in this respect according to the planets with which it is associated, or if in no conjunction, then by the sign it occupies.

Saturn indicates delays; obstacles; impediments; hidden things; fatalities; evils; dangers; it is inimical to fortune and happiness; also to marriage, women, and children; and it causes diseases.

It makes the native independent, unhappy, taciturn, envious, and miserly.

Jupiter.—Fortune; honour; success; friends; protectors; supremacy; fruitfulness.

It makes the native gay, prudent, pious, of good manners, a lover of concord, and ambitious.

Mars.—Evils caused by others; calumnies; treasons; thefts; cunning; intrigues; spoliations; strife; quarrels; wounds by fire or steel; and sometimes murders committed, or threatened.

It makes the native bold, brave, ready to anger, warlike, quarrelsome, unjust, cynical, quick to assert his own independence, inclined to litigation, and sweeping reforms.

Sun.—Elevation; honours; glory; reputation; celebrity; dignities; high offices; publicity.

It makes its subjects conscientious, just, honest, modest, courteous, clever in the knowledge of the arts, judicious, a giver of good counsel, and a lover of the truth.

Venus.—Love affairs; *liaisons*; marriage; passion; jealousy; hopes realized; joys; pleasures; protection of women of high rank.

It confers on its subjects a loving spirit, tenderness, benevolence, poesy, and a love of the fine arts.

Mercury.—All relations; science; intelligence; commerce; industries; messages; letters.

It makes the native inclined to oratory, subtile, and circumspect, suave, well-informed, inventive, and of good intellect.

Moon.—Changes; voyages; travels; all things affecting the body; mysterious things; fancies; changes of all kinds; popularity.

It renders the native inconstant, capricious, fantastic, dreamy, and inclined to fancies and sudden emotions; when dignified it is able to confer great honours by popular verdict.

The Moon and Mercury have influence over the psychic and intellectual natures; Venus and Moon over marriage, unions, and love affairs; Jupiter and Mercury over monetary matters; Mars and Sun over voyages and travels (Saturn is contrary in this matter) ; brothers and sisters are ruled by Mars. The father is signified by the 4th House, and the ruler thereof ; and the mother by the 10th and its ruler ; the affairs of the family by the 6th House and its ruler.

Very little dependence, however, must be given to the judgment which is drawn only from these planets and their affections. The Houses and Signs having affinity for the things and persons above-mentioned, must have prior consideration in coming to an accurate judgment.

Where contrary indications are seen, *changes* may be safely predicted in the matter under consideration ; as at one time the native may be poor and needy, and then come into a state of affluence because Saturn and Jupiter both give their testimony. N.B.—The planet which holds precedence in the order of the " Scale " of the Nativity will have first effect in such case.

CHAPTER IX

GENERAL RULES

PROFESSIONS.—The significators of the profession are Mars, Venus and Mercury.

Mars indicates the military arts, surgery, and occupations connected with iron and fire ; with the Sun, it denotes gold-beaters, jewellers ; with Saturn, occupations of a menial or soiling order ; with Jupiter, cabinet-makers ; wood-turners, etc. ; with Venus, butchers and coopers ; with Mercury, interpreters, administrators, etc. ; with the Moon, mariners, hydraulic engineers.

Venus denotes an aptitude to medicine and chemistry ; success in art, sculpture, music, and in dressmaking, ornamentation, personal decoration, and the like social arts. With Saturn, it denotes perfumers, cooks, and such as minister to the appetites of the body ; with Jupiter, to the physical sciences and arts.

Mercury denotes the liberal arts, letters, science, negotiations, and commerce. Opposed to Saturn it denotes servitude ; joined to Jupiter, success in oratory ; with the Sun, high occupations and government offices ; with the Moon, inventions, discoveries, and the ingenious arts which employ the intellect and imagination.

Among the Signs, Aries, Cancer, Libra, and Capricorn favour the manual arts. Gemini, Virgo, Libra, the last half of Sagittarius, and Aquarius, the liberal arts. Cancer, Scorpio, and Pisces incline to navigation.

Of the Houses : the 2nd denotes sciences having gain for their object, and such as one may call " trading." The 3rd House indicates the vocation, and the things which will afford impediments to its future. The 5th and 11th denote teachers, scientists, artists, and literary men. The 6th shows therapeutics ; the 7th, oratory ; the 9th, the priestly vocation ; the 10th, politic arts and public functions. The rulers of the profession being found in these Houses will incline to the things indicated thereby.

VIOLENT DEATHS.—The Sun or Moon, or both, in the 6th, 8th, or 12th Houses, afflicted by the malefics Saturn and Mars.

The Sun in Aries or Capricorn, and the Moon in Libra at the same time ; and one or the other of these signs in an evil house.

The Moon in Libra and Mars in the 8th house.

Sagittarius on an angle, and the Moon therein, with Mars in the 8th House.

Saturn and Mars conjoined in the 1st House, and the Moon in Sagittarius in an angle ; or if Mars be in the 8th, and Saturn rising, the Moon being so placed.

The planets Saturn, Mars, Sun, and Moon, in angles ; and Libra or Aquarius in the 1st or 8th.

These are all signs of a violent death.

Saturn afflicting, predisposes to falls ; Mars, to wounds by steel or fire, or by firearms ; the Sun, to burns ; Venus, to contagious diseases ; the Moon, to epidemics.

The significators in double signs, Gemini, Sagittarius, Pisces, and rising, denotes suicide.

The 3rd House shows death in short journeys ; or by relatives and neighbours ; the 5th or 7th females are involved, or open enemies if in the 7th. In the 10th House, death may result by the verdict of a judge, or by some person in power. In the 12th, secret enemies, obsession and melancholy causes, oftentimes when in prison, or under restraint.

In judging of the nature of the death, regard must be had also to the nature of the " element " ruled by the signs occupied by the malefics.

FORTUNE.—The 1st, 2nd, 8th, and 10th Houses, chiefly the 2nd, are to be regarded in this matter. Jupiter and Venus are the chief significators of good fortune, especially when in the Houses above-named, and in good aspect to the rulers, or themselves ruling the Horoscope. The source from which wealth or the means of livelihood will proceed is to be judged by the sign and house held by the significators. The degree of wealth will depend upon the state and affections of the significators, i.e., how it may be placed in regard to House and Sign, and how aspected.

PROGENY.—This question must be judged from the nature of the Signs and Planets occupying the 1st, 5th, and 11th Houses.

The planets which presage fruitfulness are Jupiter, Moon, and Venus. The Sun and Mercury are *neutral*, and follow the nature of the sign occupied by them. Saturn and Mars are sterile. Among the Signs, Sagittarius, Pisces, Taurus, Libra, and Cancer are fruitful. Jupiter and the Sun are masculine, Venus and the Moon are feminine. The sex of the progeny are judged by the planets promising offspring, and the signs they occupy, viz.: fire and air give masculine, water and Earth feminine. A fruitful planet in a sterile sign ; or the reverse, a sterile planet in a fruitful sign, shows abortion, or early death.

SICKNESS.—This is judged from the affections of the ruling sign, Sun and Moon ; the 6th House, its ruler, and planets in the 6th. Likewise, the signs occupied by the malefics Saturn and Mars. The parts of the body ruled by the signs being known to every initial student in the science of horoscopy, it is needless to repeat them here. If the planets signifying sickness are in the 1st House, then the maladies will ensue in the early part of life, i.e., infancy ; in the 10th, during the middle of life ; in the 7th, at full age ; and in the 4th, in old age.

CHAPTER X

LUNAR POINTS

WHAT now follows is ot the utmost importance in the determination of all questions upon which the horoscope may be consulted. Lunar Points are certain points set off from the place of the Moon in the Scale of the Nativity, and which, falling in the different Houses of the Horoscope, yield a certain and definite resolution of questions upon which even the rules heretofore given afford insufficient or doubtful evidence.

To calculate these points observe the age of the Moon at the time of birth. If the Moon be going to the full, then calculation is made from the Sign Aries. If the Moon has passed the full, then Libra must be taken as the starting point.

The MOON'S AGE.—This may be found by the following rules:—

TABLE OF CONSTANTS

January	0	May	2	September ..	7
February.. ..	1	June	3	October.. ..	7
March	0	July	4	November ..	9
April	1	August ..	5	December ..	9

(1.) Divide the year of birth by 19, multiply the remainder by 11, and divide the result by 30. This will give the Epact for the year. Then :—

(2.) To the Epact, add the day of month, and the *constant* for the month (taken from the above table). Divide the result by 30. The remainder is the Moon's age.

Example.—Required, the Moon's age on 7th July, 1856.

$$1856 \div 19 = 97 + 13$$

$$\frac{13 \times 11}{30} = \frac{143}{30} = 4 + 23 \text{ Epact.}$$

$$\frac{23 + 7 + 4}{30} = \frac{34}{30} = 4 \text{ days.}$$

Of course, the Moon's age may more conveniently be extracted from a calendar or almanac for the year of birth, but these not being always ready to hand, and inaccessible in the case of remote years, the above rules may be useful.

DURATION OF LIFE.—The Lunar Point for this question is set off as follows : From the Sign Aries or Libra—according to the Moon's age at birth—count to the Sign which holds the Moon in the Scale of the Nativity. If the count start from Aries, then Taurus is called 1, Gemini is called 2, Cancer is called 3, and so on. The number thus obtained points out the *House* where the " Lunar Point " falls.

Thus in the case of Mr. Gladstone, the Moon at birth was going to the conjunction with the Sun. The count, therefore, is from Libra. The Moon does not occur as a figure in the Scale of the Nativity, and is therefore taken to be in its own Sign, Cancer, in the 7th House of the figure. From Libra to Cancer is a matter of 9 Signs, and the "Lunar Point" will therefore be in the 9th House; where we find Jupiter and Mercury conjoined in the Sign Virgo in Trine to a confirmatory benefic aspect in the 1st House, and Jupiter throwing a ray into the 4th House. The significator Mercury being so well placed and aspected is a sign of long life. In general the following rules may be taken: (1) the sign of the Zodiac found at the Lunar Point; (2) planets good or bad there; (3) the good or bad aspects of other planets to that point; (4) the condition of the lord of that point.

THE POINT OF DEATH.—To find this Lunar Point, count from the place of the Moon in the horoscope, i.e., its *first* place in the Scale of Nativity, to the 8th House, and the number thus obtained must be counted again from the place of Saturn; and that will be the Fatal Lunar Point. From the affections of this place the *Kind of Death* is judged.

N.B.—In all these cases it is understood that the *first* place of the planets in the Scale of Navitity is to be taken as that from or to which calculation is to be made, as directed. Also it is necessary to count the signs *between* the significators, i.e., the sign from which count is made is not called 1, but the succeeding sign is so called. Thus from the Moon's sign to the 8th House, in the figure of Mr. Gladstone, is 1 sign; and one from. Saturn is Scorpio, which is the Lunar Point ruling over the Kind of Death.

When the Point falls in the 1st House it is a sign of death by one's own hand, or by faults which incur the penalty of Death; in all cases it indicates imprudence which brings death in its train as a direct consequence; and if testimonies of violence occur then it will be by execution, assassination, or suicide.

HEALTH.—In an *evening* horoscope, i.e., between mid-day and midnight, the Lunar Point for this question is counted from Jupiter to Saturn; in a *morning* horoscope, from Saturn to Jupiter. The number thus obtained indicates the House wherein the Point falls. Thus in Gladstone's figure, which belongs to the morning, count is made from Saturn to Jupiter; the planets being found in the 10th and 12th respectively, which gives 2 signs, we place the Lunar Point in the 2nd House.

THE POINT OF FORTUNE.—In evening horoscopes, from Sun to Moon; in morning ones, from Moon to Sun. Thus: From the Moon-Sign, i.e., Cancer (there is no representation of the planet itself in this horoscope) to the place of the Sun counts 11 Signs. The Lunar Point of Fortune falls therefore in the 11th House.

THE MARRIAGE POINT.—Female horoscopes count from Venus to Saturn. Male horoscopes count from Sun to Venus.

PROGENY.—Evening horoscopes count from Jupiter to Saturn; morning horoscopes from Saturn to Jupiter.

TRAVELLING.—Count in all cases from the place of the Ruler of the 9th House, to the Sign of the 9th House. The number thus obtained gives the House where the Lunar Point falls. In Mr. Gladstone's case it falls in Leo in the 8th House.

VOYAGES BY SEA.—Evening horoscopes count from Saturn to Cancer ; morning ones, the reverse. The number obtained indicates the House of the Lunar Point. From Cancer to Saturn in the figure before us is 3 signs. The Point therefore falls in the 3rd House in Pisces, with Venus, Jupiter, and Mercury therein.

FRIENDSHIPS.—Count from the Moon to Mercury in all cases. This indicates the House in which the Point falls.

ENEMIES.—In evening horoscopes count from Lord of 12th to the 12th House : in morning horoscopes the contrary, viz.: from the 12th House to its Lord.

DANGERS AND PERILS.—In evening horoscopes, from the Lord of 6th to the 6th House ; in morning horoscopes, from the 6th House to its Lord.

INHERITANCE, LEGACIES, ETC.—In either morning or evening figures the count is made from the place of Saturn to the Moon.

STATE OF MARRIAGE.—The question of accord or disaccord in the marriage state is judged from the Lunar Point, which in evening horoscopes is counted from Mars to Jupiter, and in morning horoscopes from Jupiter to Mars.

The aspects to the Lords of these Lunar Points, and the planets attending the Points, will yield the most faithful presages if properly judged. Observe that the " rays " from a planet do not count as the planet itself, and all the above " counts " are made from the bodies of the planets, and from their first positions in the Horoscope. Thus in the figure of Mr. Gladstone, Saturn is in the 10th House ; Jupiter in the 12th, Mars in the 7th, Sun in the 6th, Venus in the 3rd, Mercury in the 1st, and the Moon (not being represented in the figure) is in the 7th where its own sign is found.

The Sun and Moon having but one house each, there can be no doubt as to where they will fall when not represented in the figure ; but in the case of the planets, which have each 2 Houses, the following rule must be observed, should any of them not fall in the Scale of the Nativity.

In an evening horoscope the planets are to be taken as in their feminine or nocturnal signs.

In a morning horoscope the planets are taken as being in their masculine or diurnal signs.

CHAPTER XI

JUDGMENT BY POSITION

THE simple natures of the planets and their effects upon the character and fortunes being already known, it is a matter of practice and experience only to cover all the possible combinations of the planetary bodies, and to determine the modifications which any planet will undergo when placed in one or another of the signs, or conjoined to another planet. As the chemist, when dealing with his simple bodies, is able by experience to predicate what will result from their combinations, so the artist in Astrology, by knowing intimately the simple natures of the planets, can by experience determine what will be the result of their operations when acting in a compound or complex manner.

Primarily, the planets act in two ways: (1) by position, and (2) by aspect. The first of these needs some special consideration, since it is the key to the more complex interpretations of the astrological art. Supposing the Sun to be in the 2nd House in the Sign Sagittarius, we have several distinct data from which to make our deductions. Thus :—

1. Sun in the Sign of Jupiter ;
2. Sun in the House of Venus ;
3. Sun in a Common Sign ;
4. Sun in a Sign of Fire.

It will thus be understood that the things ruled by the 2nd House will, in this case, be under the combined influence of Sun and Jupiter ; and as these two planets act well when in conjunction, and Jupiter is in harmony with the nature of Venus, the affairs of the 2nd House may be taken as well-established and fortunate. The modifications due to evil aspects to the planets of the Sun would therefore avail but slightly to disestablish this good foundation ; while the benefic aspects would serve only to enhance and confirm it.

The significators must therefore be carefully considered after this manner, and final judgment drawn from the testimony of the Lunar Points.

CHAPTER XII

PLANETS IN THE TWELVE SIGNS

SATURN.

In *Aries*, gives troubles in marriage, obstacles in the career, perils from which the native hardly escapes, sometimes when travelling ; and this chiefly in the years of Saturn. Some inheritance after the 30th year. Hindrances in the career, and assaults upon the honour. It gives a touchy temper. Sometimes the native marries an elderly person.

In *Taurus*, he is fortunate in some degree. At first the fortunes are precarious, but afterwards improve. A lover of solitude. A careful nature, but kind. Some losses. Troubles and perils in the 9th, 14th, 25th, and 32nd years. Troubles through females. In the 8th or 12th Houses, death of the father is probable. The native may over-feed himself. Troubles in love affairs, and through children. Contagious diseases.

In *Gemini*, few or no children, or sickness to them in infancy. Mechanics, inventions. Troubles about the 23rd year, and in those ruled by Saturn. An ingenious nature. Energy and force of character. Persecutions from persons jealous of the native's position and property. Aptitude for scientific work. Faculty of observation.

In *Cancer*, intelligence and will-power. Damage to property. Difficulties in travelling, and in the occupation of houses. Discord and strife on all sides. Premature loss of parents. Dangers to the position. Danger of falls from high places, and of drowning.

In *Leo*, assaults upon the honour and position. Two marriages. Obstacles in the career by the opposition of superiors. Will-power which will surmount difficulties. Good faith, judgment, integrity. Many friends. Inheritance from the father. Reversals, loss of employment ; and if in the 12th House, captivity.

In *Virgo*, mysteries, fatalities in life. Chastity. Religious spirit. Taste for science, and philosophy Knowledge of Divine and spiritual mysteries. Misfortunes and sickness in the first part of life. Ingenuity. Overcoming of perils and obstacles by force of character. Taste for public life. Unhappiness if married to a young person, better if the partner be advanced in years. Sometimes gives two marriages.

In *Libra*, troubles and disgrace at intervals of 7 and 9 years. Study of law. Love of sciences. Obstructions. Troubles in marriage, or in one's associations. Numerous open enemies, chiefly female. Favours from superiors. Spirit of contradiction and argumentation. Nervous susceptibility. Contagious diseases. Troubles in the profession if in 10th, 6th, or 12th.

In *Scorpio*, epidemic complaints. Danger of sudden death by secret enemies or animals, especially when it is in 8th House. Drowning accidental or voluntary. Perils of magnitude. Anxieties throughout the life. Danger of an early death. The dangers to the body will not cease till the 42nd year. Plots against the native. Violent temper, sudden resolutions. Unpleasant journeys. Strife and danger therein. If benefics aspect Saturn by trine or sextile, these evils will be partly overcome.

In *Sagittarius,* injures the marriage state. Hinders fortune and success ; gives misfortune and want, poverty. In a morning horoscope it denotes dangers proceeding from the father. Prevents elevation and honours. Troubles with the wife, which may lead to separation. Causes the native to take to more than one profession at the same time. Losses. Courteous disposition. Scientific. Possible honours, but tardy.

In *Capricorn,* plans followed by deceptions, success followed by failure ; sorrows ; want of foresight ; poverty ; losses ; unhappy end to one's affairs ; much trouble and affliction. Exposure to perils ; falls ; wounds ; chronic illnesses. Gravity, prudence, melancholy.

In *Aquarius,* cannot do much for the success of the native, but gives a good disposition, grave and penetrating, which may command the support and sympathy of persons advanced in years ; in cardinal Houses it gives elevation under superiors, and through them. Makes the native slow in action and speech.

In *Pisces,* delays marriage, or causes troubles therein. Troubles in love affairs, and through children. Dangers by falls into water. Long illness. Falls from horses. Many enemies. Losses and troubles which may be overcome by perseverance. Wilful or accidental drowning. Quarrels with superiors or powerful adversaries. Dangers to the father. Secret enemies causing great perils. Loss of children.

JUPITER.

In *Aries,* wounds by military men. Success in arms, as a soldier. Military honours. Good fortune. Successful enterprises. Government employ. Gives protection in martial dangers.

In *Taurus,* difficulties and perils which will be followed by powerful friends and happy enterprises. Favours from women in position ; but dangerous relations with evil men. Strength of character, love of justice, devotion. Ingratitude of friends ; profitable associations. Wealth coming from women, or by the profession. A happy marriage.

In *Gemini,* powerful friends, help from such. Good fortune, but exposed to perils and vicissitudes, or sudden reversals towards the 45th year. Otherwise a peaceful life. Mathematical ability ; gain by negotiations and wide transactions ; benefits from inventions and industries. The native will be the eldest of his father's children, or the most capable and the foremost.

In *Cancer,* wealth in land, property, etc. ; inheritance ; powerful, but inconstant friends ; good reputation ; wealth by popularity, either in his own land or abroad. An exalted position. Safe voyages. Supremacy badly acquired.

In *Leo,* sure fortune. High interests and relationships. Good credit. Responsibilities of high order. Governmental position. Good nature, endowed with wisdom, will-power, prudence, foresight. Favours from persons in high position. Church dignities. Authority. Command. Good and rich marriage.

In *Virgo*, danger of loss through women, or secret means. A prosperous marriage. Curious benefits, or mysterious good fortune. Unforeseen gain. Honesty, fidelity, and affection. Loyalty. Aptitude for the study of science. Makes tutors, guardians of minors, etc. The wife is of a frank, honest nature ; endowed with youth, beauty, and fortune. Gives employment in the magistracy or in religious orders. Danger to the eyes. Fine children. Gives wisdom, knowledge, goodness, and honesty. Ability for close study of natural laws. Native will be richer than his parents. Sometimes a mysterious marriage.

In *Libra*, justice, fidelity, courtesy. Employment in the magistracy or government. Goodwill and support of dignitaries, after difficulties. Inheritance and gifts. Certain honours. Happy marriage, after some love affairs. Benefits from females, also from friends. Gives competence if not fortune in the latter part of life. Help from influential women.

In *Scorpio*, danger of troubles, or injury in love affairs, marriage, and by the marriage partner. Jealousy. Unhappy marriage. Treachery of friends. Many losses ; loss of inheritance ; spoliation. Premature loss of the first child. Exposed to great dangers through imprudence. Loss or wounds by military or Mars men. Liability to disgrace. Quarrels, lawsuits. Losses at play. Powerful enemies, jealous and envious opponents. Supremacy acquired by violence.

In *Sagittarius*, good rider, fond of sports, successful in use of arms. Victory over enemies ; good fortune, wealth, inheritance. Sure dignities and honours. Landed properties. Estates. Success in all things. High offices. A position in association with nobles or eminent men.

In *Capricorn*, tardy fortune, losses. A tendency to despotism, holding sway over inferiors with delight. Marriage unsatisfactory. Troubles in the birth and rearing of children. Treacherous friends. Danger of ruin in speculations. Avarice. Small ambitions.

In *Aquarius*, fortune due to the devotion and support of friends. Indifference to the ordinary interests of life, flexibility, lassitude, melancholy. Afflictions, troubles, quarrels which will be dangerous to the native. Prudence, piety, adverse to all kinds of strife and disputation. Gain by dealing in fluids, or such as have air and water as the motor powers. Marriage to a person advanced in years.

In *Pisces*, probability of two marriages. Sudden adversities before the 30th year, maybe in travelling, and maybe in financial matters. Increasing fortunes, high occupations, some honours, noble friends, command, dignities. Enmity of persons in high positions which will not harm the native. Some troubles in married life through calumnies and scandals.

MARS.

In *Aries*, irritable, quarrelsome, and litigious character, always ready to attack by word or deed. Liable to be wrongly influenced. Teasing and warlike spirit. Liable to wounds in the head. Cause of quarrels, of battles, of duels. Gives pains in the eyes and bowels. Gives proficiency in mathematics, and the strategic sciences ; sometimes raises the native to high commands.

In *Taurus*, inspires audacity, rashness, and the tendency to do every-

thing to succeed ; predisposes to submit to a female yoke, and to fall
into unavoidable misfortune. Adultery dangerous. Wounds from
wild beasts. Violent feelings. Harm to women or by women. Loss
of property.

In *Gemini*, inclines towards a taste for arms and inspires stratagems
in men who follow that career. Gives mental acuteness and prudence,
united with cunning. Makes cross-examiners, diplomatists, and clever
detectives. The native will distinguish himself by his ingenuity of
mind. · Success (for men of war). Unfortunate travels ; dangerous
wounds ; sudden and unexpected poverty ; make the native slightly
deceptive ; unforeseen dangers away from home.

In *Cancer*, favourable to those who would choose the military profession. Gives fitness for medicine and surgery. Inspires boldness,
but renders the will changeable ; not persevering in following out the
end proposed. Gives weakness of sight, and gastric derangements ;
dangers to the mother ; frivolity ; bold enterprises ; wounds from
hidden enemies.

In *Leo*, makes conquerors, commanders-in-chief, and monarchs.
Gives force of character, boldness, contempt of dangers, victory in
struggles and supremacy. Gives a tendency to gloom and gravity.
May endanger the eyes, especially the right eye. Danger of exile, of
violent death by sword or fire, far from the native country (if Mars and
the Lion are in unfortunate houses, i.e., VI., VIII., XII., or if Saturn
is in conjunction or square aspect to Mars). Death out of the father-
land. Liability to pains in the eyes and stomach. Powerful enemies.
Wounds caused by large quadrupeds.

In *Virgo*, danger of being led astray. Mysterious woundings. Unhappy, or unsuccessful in love. In the female horoscope : Probability
of marrying a military officer. Causes rather irascible and deceitful
character. Gives strange and peculiar struggles in life ; great misfortunes on account of women ; bold scientific enterprises, crowned
with success.

In *Libra*, high positions in the administration of justice. Struggles
in love. Sorrows and lawsuits on account of women. Accusation of,
and condemnation for, guilty acts (if Saturn is in bad aspect). Gives
a taste for arms, but exposes to great adversities and to serious wounds
by sword or fire. Dangers in duels or in war. Success in lawsuits.

In *Scorpio*, aggressive and warlike spirit. Great struggles in life.
Danger of violent death from hidden enemies. Treachery. Dangerous wounds. Boldness, rashness ; cynicism when the Moon and
Mercury are in bad aspect. Gives falls and acute illnesses, murders
committed or undergone (if the Moon is in conjunction with Saturn as
well, or square). Acts of violence committed on or by women (in the
VI., VIII., or XII.). But if *Jupiter* or Venus are in conjunction or
trine to *Mars*, the predicted evils are considerably reduced, and may
even give rapid military promotion. Victory over enemies ; military
prowess. The marriage partner will not be happy.

In *Sagittarius*, high military positions. Quarrels and litigation with
persons of position in regard to property. Danger of death by murder
(if the Moon is in conjunction with *Mars*, or in the I., IV., VII., or X.
Houses). Dangers through surgical operations or medical error.
Wounds by quadrupeds in the chase, or otherwise. Renders the native
inactive in the early part of life.

In *Capricorn,* great struggles in life. Dangerous wounds. Makes the native brave and bold, loving heroic adventures, and regardless of peril ; gives success by acts of bravery. Gives dangerous and deceitful enemies. Premature death of brothers. Danger of falls, or of acute diseases. Predisposes to favours and friendships of powerful men, perhaps military. Danger of violent death by drowning.

In *Aquarius,* inclines to *evil* and to want of *good faith,* violent quarrels, crimes (if Saturn afflicts). Audacity and enterprise. Fatal strife. Danger of falls, or acute diseases, weakness or pains in the legs. Gives encounters with violent people. Outrages. Premature loss of brothers. Deception by false friends, aged persons, or learned men. Causes blind and secret animosity. Seeking to injure by base intrigues and calumnies. Liability to dangerous wounds by the hand of man. Some danger on water, or by acts of bravado.

In *Pisces,* great struggles to acquire the means of maintenance or fortune. Harmful calumnies on the part of high functionaries. Always harmful to marriage ; separating or destroying. Denies children or afflicts them. Gives troubles in love affairs. Evils to the wife, mother, sisters, and all females of the family. In female horoscopes renders the marriage sterile. Causes poverty ; but promises goodwill and support of high personages. High military positions. This aspect ennobles. Natural timidity capable of changing suddenly to audacity ; wounds to the feet or hands. Passionate nature. The family will be harmful, and liable to cause wounds to the native.

SUN.

In *Aries,* gives high office in the army or magistracy. Variable fortune. Alternate elevation and abasement. Voyages with or for high personages, or on some sort of mission. Much advancement. Dignities. Honours. Celebrity. Renown. Gives probity and good morality.

In *Taurus,* increase of fortune. Some disputes or lawsuits in regard to marriage. An observant mind. Knowledge, and meditative mind. Aptitude in the occult sciences. Love of travel.

In *Gemini,* gives ballooning and mountain climbing ; favours the pursuit of science, which will yield, however, little profit. Good judgment. Small fortune ; perhaps loss of wealth. Promotion in life due to help from brothers, relatives, or friends.

In *Cancer,* many enemies ; much sorrow ; much travel. Complaints of the stomach. Danger in the water (if Saturn or Mars is in bad aspect). This position may give captaincies of ships travelling long distances ; admirals, or genuine marines. It helps the native to triumph over jealous persons, and enemies of low position in life.

In *Leo,* gives much promotion ; proud self-confidence ; aptitude for science, philosophy ; love of all that is fine, good, just, and true ; honours and wealth (especially in good houses, i.e., I., II., III., V., X., XI.) ; successful travels ; advancement ; high office ; favours ; happiness and success in love ; but some dangers in regard to marriage, children, or position (when *Saturn* or *Mars* is in evil aspect).

In *Virgo,* impediments by some mysterious relationships. Secret missions. High grades in freemasonry. Gives high position in police service ; men in whose hands are the invisible threads which move the whole of society. Gives occult powers ; celebrity (good or bad according to the aspects) ; inclination to divinity, theology, spiritualism, astrology, magic. This aspect confers the highest intellectual gifts. Knowledge with modesty, discernment with goodwill conduces to large and useful undertakings, and to sudden advancement. Wealth and honour in middle life. Reputation through knowledge.

In *Libra*, good moral qualities. Position in life uncertain. Good conscience. Separation in marriage ; threatens a life apart from one's children. Gives a contemplative mind ; artistic or poetical abilities. May overthrow the highest positions (if *Saturn* or *Mars* is in bad aspect). Gives aptitude in the natural sciences ; love of truth and of the beautiful ; spirit of observation ; interested in the secrets of nature. Gives a love of travel and of the country ; liability to condemnation ; love of equity ; aptitude for legislation.

In *Scorpio*, discovers the snares of enemies. Gives the enmity of high personages ; dangers beyond the seas, either from savages, venomous reptiles, or marsh fevers ; danger of sudden death by sword, fire, or lightning (all this in bad houses, i.e., VI., VIII., and XII.) ; blindness in favourable houses, and in good aspect to Jupiter. The Sun in Scorpio may give reputation, celebrity, sympathy of great people; but these good conditions will not last (Scorpio being the most harmful sign of the Zodiac). Inspires love of self ; exaggerated pride, or of wounded dignity, which will create enemies and cause many changes in the sphere of life.

In *Sagittarius*, give high positions and honourable dependencies ; love of show, ostentation, and luxurious surroundings. Threatens premature loss of children ; spoils marriage. Gives ardent passions, superiority or nobility, and honour above all relatives ; painting and sculpture ; dangers from hidden enemies (in an evening horoscope).

In *Capricorn*, gives overthrow of positions ; heart disease ; short life (if *Jupiter* is not in good aspect). The honour will suffer through evil associations. Renders the native careful in his actions, prudent in counsel, and undertaking nothing rashly. May give a certain degree of celebrity, good or bad (according to the position of *Jupiter* in the figure) ; varying health.

In *Aquarius*, gives a certain elevation, although somewhat slow ; dangers to the position, and fluctuating honours. Celebrity by the physical sciences, long life, enmities among persons of rank. Reputation through occult things. Rare and eccentric faculties. Makes *illuminati*, ascetics, theurgists, etc. Gives popular success in architecture, painting, sculpture, or political science.

In *Pisces*, gives high office, not likely to endure ; uncertain position ; arrogance, haughtiness, tyrannical, will undergo anything, and resist everything in order to accomplish its desires, hence terrible strife against fatality. High ambitions ; thirst for glory. Makes monarchs and · chiefs of states. Illness, or dangers to children. Premature loss of the eldest child probable. Noble and rich marriage, but little happy. Powerful secret enemies who will cause downfall. Gives wealth by employment and in church affairs. The native will take precedence over his brothers. Danger of violent death by secret enemies. Liability to watery diseases, e.g., dropsy, diabetes, etc.

VENUS

In *Aries*, the native will marry young. Gives cares and sadness; dangers in love, e.g., seduction. Sometimes prevents or spoils marriage. Gives dangers for or through women. Renders character fickle. Gives unhappy marriage (in the case of women).

In *Taurus*, gives happiness, the realization of hopes, success in undertakings; some troubles in love. Renders the native voluptuous. Gives riches coming from women by marriage, heritage, or legacy.

In *Gemini*, gives goodness, wisdom, inventive mind; troubles in love; tendency to jealousy; fine children; birth of twins probable (in female horoscope). The native will be involved in a dual marriage relationship.

In *Cancer*, gives fickle affections; separations; divorces; marriage to an aged person, or to one divorced; variable fortune; marriage abroad, or to a foreigner. Renders the native of light character. Gives dangers in love, e.g., seduction; inconstancy; marriage union while travelling. Gives many children.

In *Leo*, successful marriage; happiness through the marriage partner; elevation through the influence of a lady of position; good reputation; favours of the great. Superior nature. The subject will both love and marry early.

In *Virgo*, may give illicit love, but little happiness therein (if *Mars* be in bad aspect). Sometimes makes celibates, and gives a desire for monastic life. If *Saturn* is in bad aspect, gives immorality. Gives goodwill; support of churchmen; mysterious strife. The native will do harm to women.

In *Libra*, successful marriage; fortunate relationships; patronage of ladies of quality; faithful affections; happy nature; much prosperity; enjoyment of life; luck in enterprises; probable rivalries in love which may cause some enmities. Fiery passions. Some dangers owing to women.

In *Scorpio*, dangerous relations in love, and severe sorrows in consequence. Danger of death by the hand of a woman. In the case of women, liability to frailty. Proud and violent temperament, hesitating at nothing to satisfy its desires (if *Mars* is in bad aspect). Disagreements with the marriage partner; unhappy marriage (especially for women). Apt to be betrayed and disappointed in love. But if *Scorpio* is in the first House, or *Libra* or *Taurus* rising, and in bad aspect to *Mars*, the subject will do harm to women.

In *Sagittarius*, gives plurality of marriages, and hence early widowhood; goodwill of powerful personages. The native may marry a relation of some degree or other, or perhaps a foreigner. Mysterious love affairs; marriage union while travelling; enmities on account of women; immoral relations and their consequences.

In *Capricorn*, gives dangerous loves; marriage impeded; dangers through women; liability to dangerous adultery; short life; in female horoscopes, sterility; bad companions; fickle or dangerous loves.

In *Aquarius*, effeminate, and timid spirit; want of initiative; softness of character; inaptitude for strife; a calm life; danger to wife during pregnancy; late marriage; premature loss of children; unhappiness in love; secret connections; disappointed hopes; loss of wealth

D

through women ; harmful to marriage and to children.　Gives chastity, religious ideas, celibacy (in the I., III., IX.).

In *Pisces*, the native will marry young, will have a happy marriage and healthy and beautiful children, but some enmities in connection with his marriage, or harmful slanders by rivals.　Gives sometimes more than one marriage.　Science ; wisdom ; powerful intellect ; discretion ; obstinate will.　(If *Saturn* afflicts, or if the *Moon* is joined to *Venus*, then fickle loves, divorce, separation.)　Advancement by the help of ladies of quality.　Some unforeseen misfortunes in love or marriage (in evil houses).　Aptitude for the study of law.　Causes quarrels with relatives and dependents.

MERCURY.

In *Aries*, the native will be liable to condemnation for civil, military or political reasons ; he may sometimes be forced to exile himself, to fly in order to avoid proscription, condemnation, or the result of actions which render him liable to prosecution.　Gives a contentious and quarrelsome spirit ; easy speech ; greediness ; some tendency to homicide (if *Mars* is in bad aspect).　The native may fall into great misfortune, and there will be danger to the position through dangerous connections.

In *Taurus*, gives a happy disposition ; love of the table, of play, and of women ; a mind wise and capable in affairs, somewhat obstinate, headstrong, and persevering.　Gives many faithful friends ; a contemplative mind, anxieties, and obstacles ; hurts through women or in marriage ; success in the fine arts, particularly music ; acquaintanceship with women of quality ; practicability.

In *Gemini*, clever and inventive mind, capable in many things. Ability in science or literature.　Friendly relations with learned or artistic people.　Powerful mind,　Liability to trouble, to fall into poverty in the years of *Saturn* and of *Mars*.

In *Cancer*, discreet, faithful, and good nature, but somewhat changeable and flexible.　Prosperity in business, especially on rivers and the high seas.　Causes many journeys, sometimes by water.　Prevents marriage or renders it unhappy.　Gives dangerous relations with swindlers ; mind inventive, but not bringing profit to the native ; many changes of residence, country, and projects ; restless mind ; religious instincts.

In *Leo*, denotes embassies, legations, consulates, chancellorships ; frequent associations with persons of quality ; confidants of dignitaries ; a mind which seeks to govern at all cost ; taste for arms, and possibility of succeeding in that profession ; right judgment ; good memory ; scientific and poetical ability.　Gives (with the *Sun* in conjunction) occupations in which gold is dealt with, e.g., jewellers.　Also conduces to authorship, oratory ; gives sure elevation by professions, highly remunerative in accordance with the native's position.　Gives a spirit of independence.

In *Virgo*, high intellect and great knowledge.　Superior nature. Taste for literature and poetry, mathematics, strategics, and occultism. Gives inventive power, in the applied arts and powerful memory ; strength of mind and sagacity ; eloquence as orator or writer ; power of persuasion ; high order of intellect.　Makes philosophers, authors, astronomers, barristers, scholars, poets, mathematicians, and divines.

Gives a taste for mechanical industries. If *Mercury* be afflicted, adversity is almost inevitable.

In *Libra*, subordinate positions in the administration of justice; many lawsuits. Some disputes in regard to marriage, or partnerships of some sort. Just, tender, and faithful disposition. Gives useful friendships; aptitude for delicate mechanical work; mathematical sciences; inventions. Possibility of celebrity and fortune. Musical ability. Powerful and broad mind. Ability for legislation and government.

In *Scorpio*, relations with violent and outrageous persons. Evil associations and surroundings, in the VI. House, and in bad aspect to Saturn. Gives danger of some sort of poisoning. Danger of poisonous bits. In the VII. House, hidden and thoroughly harmful enmities may be expected. Corporeal dangers in strife or war (if the *Moon* be in conjunction). Gives a bold, enterprising, and reckless spirit. May afflict the tongue and voice, and cause liability to hoarseness, stammering, and (especially if *Saturn* is in conjunction with, or afflicting, *Mercury*), dumbness. In the III., VII., or IX. Houses, treacherous friendships; this also indicates condemnation and exile.

In *Sagittarius*, gives high subordinate positions, e.g., consulates, embassies, secretaryships. Indicates diplomacy, cunning; moderate success, spoiled by ingratitude of people on whom the native has conferred favours. Renders the native wise, just, prudent, and capable. Gives equity and probity, which will only meet with ingratitude. Especial aptitude for legislation and jurisprudence.

In *Capricorn*, nervous affections, e.g., epilepsy (if *Saturn* afflicts from evil houses). Gives scientific ability and intercourse with scholars, but without advantage; want of success; liability to fall into poverty and trouble (according to the house occupied by *Capricorn*); warlike spirit, good at literature and Saturnine sciences, e.g., chemistry, philosophy, divination (if Saturn is in bad aspects); restless, suspicious, cunning; cruel, and generally bad disposition.

In *Aquarius*, special ability for mathematical sciences and serious and deep studies, *e.g.*, astronomy and occult sciences. Spirit of independence. Likelihood of wealth and renown. Gives finesse, penetration, and good powers of observation and assimilations; inclination to solitude; society of learned people, aged men, and ecclesiastics. Indicates fortuitous elevation to high positions. Wealth gained by science or art. Some unexpected misfortunes through relatives. Tardy success (if *Saturn* be in X.). This position may also indicate phlegm and stolidity of character.

In *Pisces*, honourable subordinate positions. Finesse. Special ability for legislation and jurisprudence. Gain by marriage. Physical beauty. Powerful and devoted friends will assist to fortune (in XI.). Changes in employment. Ridiculous and absurd plans (if *Mars* be in bad aspect). Many chance acquaintances, whose friendship will not last long. Instability in relationships. Fruitful intellect. Numerous capabilities. Commerce on rivers or seas, or the employment of water as motive power, e.g., millers, etc. (if the *Moon* be in aspect).

MOON.

In *Aries*, danger of drowning and of mysterious woundings by women or servants. Success in life followed by some dangers. Mysterious love affairs. Adventure, some journeys with success therein. Some mysterious changes of position. Honours in public affairs. Popular success. Severe pains in the head. Powerful imagination. Fancifulness.

In *Taurus*, wisdom ; sound judgment ; sweetness ; mental vivacity ; intuition ; sympathy ; poesy ; success in business ; love intrigues ; inconstancy ; fortune helped by influential women ; increase of fortune.

In *Gemini*, excellent mental ability, but lack of prudence, and a tendency to be drawn into embarrassing positions. Inventive mind. Taste for science and art. Warm heart. Frequent travels. Good foresight. Honours and wealth. Long life. Numerous brothers and sisters. Travels in youth. Reprehensible actions in regard to marital relations.

In *Cancer*, good conscience. Great sensitiveness. Superior nature. Great obstacles in life. Hard struggles. Voyages, many, but unprofitable ; some gain therein, however, if *Jupiter* is in good aspect. Honours through hard work and a steady adherence to one's path in life. Strong imagination. Dreamy and poetical nature.

In *Leo*, this is the astral signature of the poet and man of genius. The *Moon*, which gives imagination, in conjunction with the *Sun* (*Leo* is the house of the *Sun* which gives light), makes superior natures, possessing true knowledge and omniscience. It is very rare to meet with this admirable signature. In worldly matters it gives honours through great men ; high employments ; lively and penetrating mind, and, if malefic planets afflict, it will cause instability in the position of the native.

In *Virgo*, gives peculiarity, originality, and eccentricity. Gives a taste for divination ; confers intuition, the power of " dreaming true," and presentiments. This position makes excellent somnambulists and clairvoyants. Evils resulting from inexperience or want of forethought may be expected in worldly affairs. Long life. Inconstancy in love and marriage. Travelling for strange reasons. Danger to the eyes. Knowledge of the future. Secret sorrows in the marriage state.

In *Libra*, romanesque and poetical imagination. Good conscience, uprightness and integrity. Secret love affairs. Separation. Divorce. The native may be involved in journeys to avoid the pursuit of justice or in disreputable law proceedings (if *Saturn* or *Mars* afflict). Popularity may be acquired at the bar or in the administration of justice. The fortune may be compromised by the native coming under the influence of women. Dangers to position and reputation through vindictive women, or through the native's own fault.

In *Scorpio*, the *Moon* being in its fall herein, gives bad prognostics, more particularly if *Mars* or *Saturn* afflict. Danger of premature death by violent perils, drowning, or epidemics. Evil through women. Woundings on the highway. Dangers during journeys. Short life to the mother. Mental maladies. To women, dangers in child-birth, abortions or sterility. (In evening horoscopes these dangers are lessened.)

In *Sagittarius*, well-endowed mind. Uprightness. Equity. Ability in science or letters, but slight activity, and some indifference to worldly interests, and hence danger of loss. In cardinal houses (i.e., the angles of the figure, I., IV., VII., X.) this position shortens life. On the other hand, in good houses (II., III., V., XI.) it gives long life. Advancement by the influence of women. Happy marriage, numerous children. In heritance or unexpected gifts (in II. or VIII.).

In *Capricorn*, unscrupulous and hypocritical character. The native does not meet his engagements (if *Mercury* afflicts). Indolence. Gives brain disorders, biliousness, melancholia, mania, hypochondriasis ; vitiates the secretions. Danger of wounds in war. Gives wrong views of life. Vague and indeterminate mind, given to day-dreaming. Misfortune through women ; injures marriage, and causes inconstancy. Afflicts the eyes, e.g., structural disorders and shortsightedness. Causes chest and throat disorders. But if the benefic planets are well placed, these presages are greatly modified.

In *Aquarius*, lugubrious imagination (e.g., Poe and Dante). Fretful striving after changeful projects. Strange and inexplicable terrors. Visions. Hallucinations. Liability to sorrow and a wandering life. Harm through women. Danger of alienation (if *Saturn* afflicts). Danger of very feeble sight (in VI. or XII.). Long voyages. Troubles in marriage. Popular sympathies. Unhoped for gifts from women. Frequent changes. Strange and fantastic tastes.

In *Pisces*, softness, inertia, and weakness of character. Inconstancy in love. Leaning towards adultery. Many little love affairs. Long voyages. Love of change and of travel. Sensuousness. Love of luxury. River or maritime industries. Dreamy and phlegmatic character. Loss of wealth. Fickle fortunes. Numerous brothers and sisters. Popularity acquired through travels, or in foreign lands. Mysterious enemies. Public functions. Poetical abilities. Fruitful imagination, but projects never realized. Numerous family (in feminine horoscope). Nautical tastes.

The foregoing judgments from Sign-positions will be found of great use to Astrologers in their interpretations by the ordinary or astronomical method of computing the horoscope. To a student of both systems it will be a matter of extreme interest to observe how wonderfully they corroborate one another. It need hardly be remarked that these are only general interpretations, and may be greatly modified by the relative positions and aspects of the various planets. Thus, in the case of Mr. Gladstone, whose key number 40 gives on the circle of Mercury, Moon in Virgo, the interpretation is greatly modified by the positions of Mercury and Saturn.

CHAPTER XIII

Judgment from the Thirty-one Points

In addition to the 22 Major Points, there are 9 additional ones, which, occurring in the Scale of a Nativity, need to be particularly noted. These, with their interpretations, are given in their order after the 22 Major Points :—

I.—Creative will ; acts in their beginnings ; inventions ; construction ; building up ; mysteries.

II.—Strife ; enmity ; dissension ; loss by women ; perception of high truths.

III.—Perfection in love ; harmony ; marriage ; fruitfulness ; action ; effort.

IV.—Realization ; things accomplished ; perpetuation ; establishment ; fixity ; endurance ; protection.

V.—Contests ; pain ; fire ; evil or unfortunate impulses ; anger.

VI.—Uncertainty in marriage ; danger of seduction ; irregularities.

VII.—Triumph ; honour ; glory ; reputation ; success ; victory.

VIII.—Moral liabilities ; strife ; ruptures ; separation ; breaking of ties ; dissolution ; lawsuits.

IX.—Authority and power due to merit ; acquisition of experience ; force ; wisdom ; mysteries.

X.—Elevation from a humbler position ; or fall from a high position ; reversals ; auguries ; future events.

XI.—Success in some bold enterprises ; courage ; decision ; energy.

XII.—Reversal of position ; culpability ; chastisement ; loss of honour ; danger of violent death, either enforced or voluntary ; dangers from women ; catastrophe.

XIII.—Ambitions and hopes deceived ; destruction ; undoing ; new beginnings ; death ; fatality.

XIV.—Dangers to the position through lack of initiative and decision ; danger through the force of the elements ; sexuality.

XV.—Fate ; the inevitable ; dangers to the offspring and troubles in the marriage state ; luxury.

XVI.—Overthrow ; ruin ; catastrophe ; accidents ; falls ; dangers of the elements.

XVII.—Hope, favourable, or the reverse, according to the position of this point in the horoscope ; uncertainty ; insight ; visions.

XVIII.—Crosses in love ; false sense of security ; unprofitable associations with women ; hidden perils ; treacheries ; deceptions.

XIX.—Good fortune ; successful marriage ; honours ; glory ; reputation ; happy associations.

XX.—Fatal destiny ; continual hindrances and obstacles arising in the life ; inevitable decisions ; unexpected elevation.

XXI.—Dignities ; honours ; success ; aspirations.

XXII.—Blind presumption ; success followed by loss ; entrapment ; wilful injury ; final catastrophe ; folly.

XXIII.—*Royal Star of Leo.* Protection and favour of persons in authority ; celebrity ; success.

XXVII.—*Sceptre.* Successful enterprises ; authority ; command ; creative intellect ; useful works.

XXXVII.—*Royal Star of Taurus.* Union ; marriage ; protection of ladies in position ; goodwill ; sincere friendship ; success through associations with the opposite sex.

XLIII.—*Point of the Reaper.* Destruction ; abortive enterprises ; things brought to nothing ; annihilation.

LI.—*Royal Star of Aquarius.* Fortuitous elevation ; martial tendencies ; powerful enemies ; troubles through Mars men.

LV.—*The Sword.* Triumph ; victory over difficulties ; a protection and yet a menace ; may chastise as it may confer honours ; energy.

LXV.—*Royal Star of Scorpio.* Powerful enemies ; wounds ; dangers ; gives also protection of rich persons, and a good marriage.

LXIX.—*Mars crowned.* Great fortune ; reputation ; honours by merit.

LXXI.—*The Reaper.* Dangers to the body and the interests ; executive powers.

When any of these occur in the Scale of the Nativity they must be marked in the horoscope.   The first 22 or Major Points are marked by their numbers in Roman figures ; the remaining 9 points are marked as follows :—

Royal star of Leo, ✳ in the sign Leo.
    Do.   Taurus, ✳ in the sign Taurus.
    Do.   Aquarius, ✳ in the sign Aquarius.
    Do.   Scorpio, ✳ in the sign Scorpio.

Sceptre is marked by
Reaper do.
Sword do.
Mars Crowned by   ♂ ⚌ | ∠

The above figures are marked where they occur in the horoscopes contained in this work.

As reference will be made to the annual prognostics, and the predictions derivable from these Points, and as the possible combinations of the Sum of the Horoscope for this and the next century amount to 28, the Points, XXIV., XXV., XXVI., and XXVIII., not given in the above interpretations, here follow in their order.   Those produced during the 21st century will return to the Major Points.

XXIV.—Confers the association of persons of high birth, and gives success through women of position.

XXV.—High offices under protection ; success through contest ; power acquired by experience ; the fruits of action.

XXVI.—Ruin by unfruitful enterprises, or by bad combinations ; bad use of the faculties ; money-grubbing.

XXVIII.—Rivals in enterprises ; injuries by opponents ; need of vigilance ; loss of the fruits of labour ; evil associations.

CHAPTER XIV

JUDGMENT FROM THE DECANS

THE Thirty-six Decans arise from the Division of the Twelve Signs into 3 parts each of ten degrees. The interpretations are useful, both in the horoscope and the annual prognostics. The position of the Sun in the Zodiac, or, what is the same thing, the decanate rising in the figure of the Kabalistic horoscope, must be consulted in this matter, and judgment given accordingly. Necessarily, these are only general prognostics, based upon the ruler of the Sign acting in conjunction with the ruler of the Decan, but they will often serve in helping the student to a correct judgment, and in that way are useful.

Aries. 1°—10°.—A firm and resolute character; indifferent to obstacles; proud; independent; gives success by dint of exertion and prowess.

   11°—20°.—Nobility of spirit; generosity; inclined to command and rulership; diplomatic; free and yet courteous.

   21°—30°.—Gentleness and flexibility of mind; sweetness of temper; love of pleasure.

Taurus. 1°—10°.—A highly-endowed intellect; aptitude for the pursuit of the exact sciences, mathematics, or for the legal profession; some violence or accidents in the life.

   11°—20°.—Nobility of disposition; hopeful and buoyant nature; easy rise in life to high positions; honours; eloquence.

   21°—30°.—Thwarted enterprises; dependence upon others; danger of misery and poverty; need for action and industry; independent spirit, producing troubles.

Gemini. 1°—10°.—Restless nature, which wounds itself upon every obstacle which comes in its path; danger of a violent death.

   11°—20°.—Carelessness; forgetfulness of one's interests; futility and wantonness; interest in impracticable things and useless discussions, associations, etc.

   21°—30°.—Aptitude for the subtile sciences, abstract things, and philosophies, which produce neither honour nor fortune; an anxious life; agitated mind. Catastrophes during early life.

Cancer. 1°—10°.—Vivacity of spirit; sociability; a warm, sympathetic nature, much given to social intercourse.

   11°—20°.—Tendency to abruptness, and quickness of speech and action; discourtesy; love of science and art; gives favourable chances of acquiring wealth.

   21°—30°.—Assertion of rights by force; austerity; inflexibility; sea voyages.

Leo. . 1°—10°.—Violent and ungovernable nature; strong passions; vigorous spirit; inclined to display, and having some taste for sculpture, architecture, or literature.

   11°—20°.—A phlegmatic nature; capable of resistance and much patience; self-confidence; ability for artistic pursuits; painting, design, etc. A vain nature.

21°—30°.—Several marriages ; success and honours by good luck ; inflexible, unyielding nature ; an adventurous spirit ; warlike or governmental tastes.

Virgo. 1°—10°.—Long life ; timid nature ; artistic faculty ; mechanical ability ; fond of the analytical science (theoretical or practical).

11°—20°.—An economical and orderly nature ; careful in money matters ; sober in behaviour ; patient in work.

21°—30°.—Love of speculation ; unfruitful nature ; destructive ; troubles in marriage or through relations ; inventive and speculative mind.

Libra. 1°—10°.—A just, truthful, and upright nature ; protecting the weak against the strong.

11°—20°.—Restless and ambitious nature ; worldly knowledge ; boldness ; confidence ; success in hazardous enterprises.

21°—30°.—A love of every kind of pleasure ; elegance and finery all around, and a woman in the centre. A light, flexible, and fickle nature

Scorpio. 1°—10°.—Deceptions, treacheries, and surprises in the life ; hidden and dangerous enemies ; dangerous voyages ; chimerical projects, and vain ambitions.

11°—20°.—Distrust and antipathy from superiors ; revival of old feuds and enmities ; danger of severe reversals in life ; loss of honour.

21°—30°.—Strong passions ; headstrong ; powerful will ; energy ; warlike nature.

Sagittarius. 1°—10°.—Arrogant nature ; love of independence ; success in the use of arms ; severe troubles in marriage.

11°—20°.—Religious spirit ; many strifes and contests ; dangerous passions ; self-contained nature ; scientific ability ; unlooked-for dangers. Impressionable and excitable nature ; frank.

21°—30°.—Obstinacy ; violence ; an apt nature ; cunning ; well-informed in worldly matters ; combative.

Capricorn. 1°—10°.—Dangerous travels, alternating with reversals ; troubles in love affairs.

11°—20°.—A mind given to unprofitable researches ; unrealizable enterprises ; martial tastes.

21°—30°.—A doubting, trifling nature ; impotent ; disappointed ; timid to a degree.

Aquarius. 1°—10°.—Financial anxieties, or on account of difficulty in acquiring wealth ; disappointed ambitions ; unrealized hopes ; sickness and disease contracted in the cradle or at the breast.

11°—20°.—Well-applied faculties ; sweetness of disposition ; virtuous ; courteous and obliging.

21°—30°.—Infantile sickness until the 7th year ; many serious contests during life ; many deceptions.

Pisces. 1°—10°.—Ambitious ; desiring renown ; celebrity ; bold enterprises.

11°—20°.—Indolence ; love of pleasure ; an unfruitful nature ; or one which works only fretfully and under restraint ; unfortunate.

21°—30°.—Restless nature ; confused or multifarious projects ; uncertain resolutions ; love of change and variety ; following a fantastic or impracticable career.

CHAPTER XV

ANNUAL REVOLUTIONS

IN the Kabalistic system of Astrology, judgment of future events is drawn from the annual conjunctions of the planets which conjointly rule over the horoscope and the year under consideration ; from the passage of the ruling sign into one or another of the Twelve Houses ; from the Sign which by regular procession is found to rule over the current, or any future year in the native's life ; and finally from the numerical combinations of the horoscopical "Sum," and from the disposition of the stars according to the Hermetic Circle. These methods will be explained and illustrated in their order.

As the entire pictorial and symbolic Zodiac illustrates, for those who can read its mysterious letters, the great World History ; and as the succession of the Signs illustrates the gradual unfoldment of the presage concerning human evolution which is embodied in the Zodiacal Circle ; so, in regard to the individual life, the Nativity is only a summarised "contents-sheet" of the single life, while the processional rising of the Signs indicates, more or less pointedly, the annual passage of that life's events ; as if, one by one, the leaves of the Book of Life were turned by the hand of Destiny for the instruction of the reader.

Now concerning these annual presages, take first of all the following table of

ANNUAL CONJUNCTIONS.

P.M.	☽	☿	♀	☉	♂	♃	♄	☽	☿	♀	☉	♂	♃	♄	A.M.
☉	1	8	15	22	29	36	43	50	57	64	71	78	85	92	☽
♀	2	9	16	23	30	37	44	51	58	65	72	79	86	93	☿
☿	3	10	17	24	31	38	45	52	59	66	73	80	87	94	♀
☽	4	11	18	25	32	39	46	53	60	67	74	81	88	95	☉
♄	5	12	19	26	33	40	47	54	61	68	75	82	89	96	♂
♃	6	13	20	27	34	41	48	55	62	69	76	83	90	97	♃
♂	7	14	21	28	35	42	49	56	63	70	77	84	91	98	♄

Persons born in the evening, i.e., in the period from noon to midnight, take their annual conjunctions from the column headed by the Sun (on the left side of the table) while those born A.M., i.e., from midnight to noon, take their prognostics from the right-hand column headed by the Moon.

Thus, if a person born in the P.M. (an "evening" horoscope) would know the prognostic for his 30th year of life, i.e., from the 29th birthday onwards, he will find in the above table of years one marked 30, and against this on the *left* there is Venus, and above it is Mars ; so that the prognostic must be drawn from this conjunction :—All sorts of evils proceeding from women ; sorrows of the heart ; troubles in married life ; social intrigues ; troubles in love affairs.

Had the birth been A.M., and the horoscope consequently a " morning " one, the rulers of the 30th year would have been Mercury and Mars, and the prognostic : Calumnies, dishonours ; quarrels ; new enterprises ; legal affairs ; success in mathematical and literary pursuits ; energy ; industry, etc.

The interpretations of these positions can be further extended by applying the radical rulership of the conjoined planets to the affairs of life ; as if Mars and Moon should be conjoined, then the things and affairs ruled by the house occupied by Cancer will suffer injury from martial causes or by Mars persons ; while the native will suffer also from causes related to the house occupied by Mars. This is the first of the annual interpretations.

The effects of the Conjunctions here follow in their order :—

PLANETARY CONJUNCTIONS.

Saturn and *Jupiter.*—Losses ; tardy financial success, or difficulties in business ; thwarts the good which the position of Jupiter may promise ; however, there will be success in landed property, inheritances, and the like. The native gains honours, but at some cost to himself. Has some post of honour conferred on him, or a responsible situation. Good fortune in the end, attended with local honours.

Saturn and *Mars.*—Thwarted ambitions ; difficulties in undertakings ; enterprises fall through ; dangers according to the ruling sign, and that held by Saturn and Mars. Deferred hopes. Loss of courage. Premature loss of relatives.

Saturn and *Sun.*—Loss of inheritance ; dangers in the life ; troubles in the acquisition of wealth ; increased mental powers ; danger of reversals.

Saturn and *Venus.*—Inconstancy ; troubles in domestic affairs, married life, etc. ; danger of losing a child, especially if a daughter ; Obstacles in love affairs ; delay in marriage. Some fatality in love affairs.

Saturn and *Mercury.*—Concentration of mental powers, gravity, discretion. Tendency to scientific pursuits ; intelligence conducive to success. Independent spirit ; difficulties in monetary affairs at first. Undertaking serious studies.

Saturn and *Moon.*—Mental disorders, and some affection of the urinary ducts. Adversity. Danger of drowning. Troubles in domestic life ; may be loss of wife or mother. Danger during voyages. The native becomes careful in money matters, and has need to be so. Mechanical inventions will succeed. Dangerous illness, or a fall from a high place. With females, bad for child-birth. Inclines to suicidal thoughts, if the nativity shows it.

Jupiter and *Mars.*—Military honours, or success in any martial occupation, in government and public functions. Favours voyages and law proceedings. Gives industry and speculations conducing to success.

Jupiter and *Sun.*—Gives a rise in the position of the native ; gain ;

honours, according to the station in life. Celebrity or good reputation. Industry and morality.

Jupiter and *Venus.*—Favour and support of high personages, especially women ; gain ; inclination to love affairs or marriage. Happiness, tranquillity, and steady progress in the life.

Jupiter and *Mercury.*—Tendency to judicial or ecclesiastical work. Clerical, literary, or professional honours ; scholastic success. Prudence ; discretion ; devotion to duties and to the means of advancement ; gives the love of children ; gain by one's works, and the use of the faculties ; ambition.

Jupiter and *Moon.*—Inclines to religion ; to success in public life ; gives happy voyages or beneficial changes ; health ; friends ; gain in whatever occupation is followed. Favours from ladies of rank or fortune.

Mars and *Sun.*—Difficulties in the career ; afflictions ; treacheries. Danger of wounds by iron or fire ; or of grave burnings. The mind is vacillating and unstable, of no fixed resolutions, yet inclined to some bold enterprises. Danger to the sight, especially the right eye. Military success, if the occupation be of that nature.

Mars and *Venus.*—Discords, embarrassment, and disputes occasioned by females ; troubles in love affairs, in the married life or the home ; injuries and calumnies ; contagious affections of the body. passionate impulses. If married, danger of separation, or grave dishonours.

Mars and *Mercury.*—Quickened intellect and increased efforts. Success in active enterprises ; but some danger of being cheated. If the nativity shows it, the native will incline to nefarious practices at this time.

Mars and *Moon.*—Inclination to the practical arts ; engineering, etc., but without much profit. Many journeys, and perhaps a voyage. Danger to the eyes, especially the left. Danger of serious wounds. Violent tendencies ; fevered mind and body.

Sun and *Venus.*—Gain and reputation. Fortune favoured by the assistance of women of position or means ; honours ; and happiness. The native inclines to marriage, and may do so to advantage. Friendship and confidence are given to the native. Position will be influenced by women, and greatly helped thereby.

Sun and *Mercury.*—The use of the faculties conduce to fortune. The native strikes out some useful plans, and may succeed in their development. Inclination to literature ; intellectual pursuits. Advancement in the occupation. Gives new friendships.

Sun and *Moon.*—Gives obstacles in marital relations. Troubles in the social and business position by means of females. Danger to the eyes (if Saturn or Mars be in evil aspect). Brain disorders ; bad fevers. Illness. New relations and enterprises, attended with success and honour. Promotion. Dangers in voyages and journeys by drowning or accident of other kind. Inventive faculties are now aroused.

Venus and *Mercury.*—Errors of judgment. Troubles by jealousy. Passion. Pleasures of all kinds attract the native ; and the more effeminate qualities of the nature are stimulated. The native is disposed to the study of light arts ; may incline to the drama. Gives a taste for dress and female society. Some troubles through women.

Venus and *Moon.*—Troubles in the domestic life, in love, or marriage. Danger of unfaithfulness. The native is light and fickle in his conduct. Removes his affection from one to another object. The wife or partner causes trouble, and may be subject to dishonours. The native inclines to pleasures more than usual at this time of life.

Mercury and *Moon.*—Activity of mind ; scientific studies ; poetical faculty or literary taste stimulated. Success in studies and profession. Right use of the faculties conducive to reputation. Nautical tastes, love of travelling by water. Good credit.

N.B.—It will be observed that these prognostics are of the most general nature only ; and must needs be, since much depends upon where the significators are placed in the Annual figures, as to what interpretation should be placed upon them. It will further be seen that the interpretations are not repeated for Jupiter and Saturn, as for Saturn and Jupiter, these being the same. Should the conjunction for the year involve a planet which is the ruler of the Annual figure, much attention must be given to its companion planet, its nature, position in the radical and annual figures, etc. ; for it is then a more remarkable significator of the native's fortunes.

The next method of judgment is from the passage of the ruling Sign into the different Houses in succession. The Zodiac is presumed to advance one sign annually, the ruling sign being carried from the 1st House into the 12th, 11th, 10th, etc. To find the place of the ruling or natal sign at any age, consult the following table :—

Natal Sign in I.	at following ages :—		1	13	25	37	49	61	73
,, XII.	,,	,,	2	14	26	38	50	62	74
,, XI.	,,	.	3	15	27	39	51	63	75
,, X.	,,	,,	4	16	28	40	52	64	76
,, IX.	,,	,,	5	17	29	41	53	65	77
,, VIII.	,,	,,	6	18	30	42	54	66	78
,, VII.	,,	,,	7	19	31	43	55	67	79
,, VI.	,,	,,	8	20	32	44	56	68	80
,, V.	,,	,,	9	21	33	45	57	69	81
,, IV.	,,	,,	10	22	34	46	58	70	82
,, III.	,,	.,	11	23	35	47	59	71	83
,, II.	,,	,,	12	24	36	48	60	72	84

This means that the ruling sign at birth passes into the 12th House on the 1st birthday anniversary, and during the 2nd year continues therein. A proportion at the rate of 4 months for each Decan can be made, so that if the last Decan of a sign were rising at birth, then in something less than 4 months afterwards, the sign of the Nativity would pass into the 12th House. But at the 2nd birthday, and the 14th, 26th, etc., it will be found in the 12th House, and as much advanced therein as at birth it was advanced in its rising in the 1st House. Hence, during any one year of life the ruling sign may be passing through two successive houses ; and the following prognostics must be regulated thereby.

PASSAGE OF RULING SIGN
INTO

XII.—Troubles which are difficult to overcome. Obstacles and hindrances in all affairs. Sickness. Bad for travelling, for opening negotiations, or for engaging in contests. Treachery among supposed friends. Mental troubles, sorrows, and persecutions.

XI.—Anxieties ; danger of losing one's good name and reputation ; difficulties in one's undertakings ; checks in fortune by secret enemies ; but support and assistance from devoted friends and colleagues. Short journeys, voyages, or change of position most probable.

X.—Good success in enterprises, which will augment or give rise to fortune. Good for journeys by sea, and for conquest of enemies. Good reputation ; fair hopes. Possibility of marriage. Family mourning.

IX.—Good year for travelling. Good for associations of love or friendship. Good for high patronages and enterprises. Liability to loss of reputation by some scandal.

VIII.—Illness ; danger of death. Treason of friends ; injurious love affairs. Friends become enemies and give rise to strife.

VII.—Danger from robbery or fire. Good year for marriage. Disagreement with relations. Disgrace in the eyes of superiors. Great change in position.

VI.—Dangerous sickness. Heavy contests and strifes. Lasting and dangerous enmities. Moderate success. Distrustful of all, and distrusted also. Great need of watchfulness. Bodily dangers, wounds, and contusions.

V.—Danger of treachery and unfaithfulness, but probable good fortune ; creditable associations ; favours from superiors ; opportunity for marriage ; providential help ; employment gives rise to fortunate voyages.

IV.—Legacy or gift. Danger of loss or of drowning ; shipwreck. Fortunate year for personal enterprises. Family journeys. Opposition in love affairs.

III.—Year of travelling, or more or less changes of residence. Danger of permanent hatred and secret diseases. Disgrace in the eyes of superiors. Loss of wealth, and of friends ; followed by envy and malice. The position is unfortunate.

II.—Good year for pecuniary interests, but danger of being robbed. Friends become enemies. Danger from quadrupeds, horses, cattle, etc. The position is favoured by influential patrons. Possibility of undertaking long voyages. Bodily dangers for the marriage partner.

I.—When the ruling sign passes into the 1st House, judgment must be made by the relation of the signs to the houses which they are normally associated with, as well as by their inherent natures and significations.

The next means of deriving the annual prognostics is from the rising of the Signs by procession. The foregoing method presumes that the ruling sign passes from one house to another ; this necessarily brings the signs in succession to the 1st House, and from this rising the prognostics are drawn, in general terms, as follows :—

PROCESSIONAL RISING OF THE SIGNS.

When *Aries* comes into the 1st House, there will be danger of wounds or of some sort of dislocation ; sickness ; sorrows ; mourning. Release from enemies. Gain or benefits by associations and alliances, whether private or in business affairs. Danger of losing the position held by the native on account of his own fault, or through the interposition of friends and associates. Contests and strife among relatives. Short journeys by the family, or on their account, for some secret purpose ; not very satisfactory. Sickness due to irregularities in the bowels. Marriage or some close association of interest. Danger by water, or some casualty of a serious nature. Good year for love affairs. Loss of friends. Expected legacies or inheritance will be realized. Harmful journeys. Triumph over enemies. A bad year for persons born under Virgo, Scorpio, or Pisces.[1]

When *Taurus* rises ; heavy quarrels. Sickness. Difficulties in business and in love affairs. Helpful friendships and patronage, but followed by misunderstandings. Help from some relative or member of one's own family. Hidden enemies affect the position. Short journeys, changes of residence or of locality. Evils through women ; loss of friends by death or by the rupture of their friendship. Loans to friends and investments of trust do not come duly to hand. The native may be imposed upon. Separation or divorce imminent, if the nativity shows it. Bad for persons born under Libra, Sagittarius, or Aries.

When *Gemini* rises ; danger of falls. Unstable position. Danger of wounds and of mourning. Considerable gain, and other benefits will be realized. Good fortune or honours to relatives. Material tendencies. Danger to the body. Strife among friends. Possibility of marriage. Illness is almost certain. Troubles in love, or wounded affections. Unlooked-for enmities. Love affairs or some close relationship will create troubles, and may cause strife and so injure the interests. Gain, which will, however, be dissipated or lost very soon. Bad year for those born under Scorpio, Capricorn, or Taurus.

When *Cancer* rises ; honours of some magnitude. Elevation. Beneficial changes. Danger to children (by wounds or martial ailments). Establishes the position. Love affairs impeded or frustrated by relatives. New acquaintances among the learned or the clergy. Evil through women. Sickness or accident to the marriage partner. Grief ; mourning. Danger in business partnerships and associations ; or through the wife in regard to money. Secret enemies ; treachery. Quarrels and misunderstandings with relatives. Help from friends and patrons. Rivalries. Loss of property and money ; or property may be seriously injured. Bad for persons born under Gemini, Sagittarius, or Aquarius.

When *Leo* rises ; affairs will necessitate short journeys. Some financial loss during such travels. Harmful enterprises. Harm from friends in matters of money and property. Trouble through children. Family suffering. The position will greatly prosper, or the reverse. A death will be profitable to the native. Serious losses by gaming or by speculation, if indulged in. It will be necessary to avoid yachting, boating, and bathing under dangerous circumstances, for there is some indication of drowning. The wife (or husband) will be sick or afflicted by troubles. The placing of affections will create enmities in the native's life during this time. Hidden enemies will seek to injure the position. Distrust of servants. Bad for persons born under Capricorn, Pisces, or Cancer.

When *Virgo* rises ; the position is difficult, and sometimes dangerous. Powerful and declared enmities arise, but they will not seriously

---

[1] Observe that this is the Kabalistic, and not the astronomical "rising sign."

affect the native. New enterprises, novel ideas applied to practice. Inclination to marriage, but instability therein. Danger to children by water. Loss of friends or relatives. Benefits by an alliance of some sort. Love affairs of a harmful nature. Secret affairs in regard to marriage or partnerships. Sickness arising from excess, or from unhealthy environment. Conjugal discord. Some corporeal dangers by strifes, wars, etc. Bad for persons born under Aries, Leo, Capricorn, or Aquarius.

When *Libra* rises ; danger of death by secret enemies. The family renders much service to the native. Danger of corporeal hurts. Fortunate associations due to the partner. Material tendencies, inordinate appetites. Relatives create strife. Good health. Instability in the position. Treacheries. Bad for persons born under Pisces, Virgo, or Taurus ; Pisces above all.

When *Scorpio* rises ; elevation assured position. Honours. Love affairs, or marriage. Affections of the head. Long voyages, and dangers resulting therefrom. Patronage of ladies of position. Change of residence leading to strife, wounds, or sickness. Secret love affairs injure relatives. New associations. Unavoidable strifes and sorrows of which the native will be the cause. Danger of drowning. Persecutions by declared enemies, or by the partner. Separation, divorce. Affairs hindered by secret enemies. Malevolent relatives will injure the native's interests or his affections. Changes, harmful to the career. Benefits by scientific affairs, by secret discoveries, or things having regard to sea voyages. Bad for persons born under Aries, Gemini, Cancer or Libra.

When *Sagittarius* rises ; danger of falls from high places, or loss of position. Financial loss, due to the native himself or his relatives. Gain or benefits by friendly relations. Obstacles in love affairs. Occupation suffers by death. Position strained through engagements with rivals or declared enemies. Conjugal discord or separation. Unforeseen benefits, inheritance or gifts. Grave illness. Unhealthy relationships. Secret love affairs. Danger to the marriage partner. Sickness of children. Relationships productive of strife. Gain by hardy enterprises, or success in litigation. Changes. Bad for persons born under Taurus, Cancer, or Scorpio.

When *Capricorn* rises ; new ambitions. Lucrative enterprises. Success in the profession or one's affairs. Long journeys and sea voyages should be shunned, being evil and dangerous at this time. Association with scholars or travellers. Change of residence. Short journeys leading to disappointments. The native may undertake journeys to bring about marriage ; but, if married, may expect conjugal discord. Friendships newly acquired, which the native will do well to be cautious about. If marriage occur at this period, it will be more lucrative than well-assorted. Some association which will bring benefits, but these will not endure. Secret or unseen hindrances in the affairs of the native. It is necessary to be careful of quadrupeds, particularly horses, and those who tend them. Servants and underlings create dangers. Danger of accidental poisoning, either in food or medicine. Bad for persons born under Gemini, Leo, or Sagittarius.

When *Aquarius* rises ; the affairs will cause many short journeys. Benefits are sure but not lasting. Affections of the head, brain, or chest. Danger of wounds, or hurts by fire and iron. Position unstable. Long journeys leading to a reversal of position. Wealth and property is seriously affected by secret enemies or travels. Harmful associations. Dangerous occupations, or pursuits, liable to bring death in their train. Harmful changes in the affairs. Machinations of secret enemies, traps, snares. A very dangerous period. Danger from horses. Enduring persecutions, driving the native into positions more or less hopeless. Danger to children. Physical dangers caused by one's self on water, or in relation with that element. Serious enmities, which, however, will pass away with the sign. Sorrow and trouble to relatives. Bad for persons born under Cancer, Virgo, or Capricorn.

When *Pisces* rises; the position and occupation are benefited. Misunderstandings with some friends, which it is desirable to pass over. Some sorrows caused by slander. Changeful affections. Physical excesses. Treachery of friends, and losses through them. Dangerous illness (if the heart or stomach are attacked). Danger of death among relatives. Contests in regard to marriage; open enmities. Travelling is certain. Separation, divorce. Unstable affections. The position is endangered by false friends, failing patrons, or others who will certainly deceive. Troubles through relatives. Troublesome journeys. Bad for persons born under Leo, Libra, or Aquarius.

It will be observed that the above general prognostics are subject to the same modifications and considerations as were applied to the " Passage of the ruling sign " in the previous section of this chapter. If, for instance, the 20th degree of a sign were rising at birth, the prognostics for that sign will continue to hold for 4 months only, and then the influence passes to the next sign, and the succeeding 8 months exhaust two-thirds of the sign. In general it may be remarked that the rising of these signs in the horoscope is subject to the same interpretation, although in an extended sense, applicable to the whole life instead of a current year merely. In this sense they will be found doubly useful.

The next method of prognostication is from the key number of the Nativity, when added to the year under consideration, and extended in a Kabalistic manner.

KEY NUMBER OF NATIVITY.

This is the extended sum of the figures resulting from a computation of the Christian and surnames, the sign of birth and the degree of birth. If this be added to the year under consideration it gives the " Sum of the Revolution " of the Nativity. Thus, it was found that the sum of the Nativity of Mr. Gladstone's case was 40. To get the prediction for the year 1894 we proceed thus :—

$$1894$$
$$40$$

$$1934 = 1 + 9 + 3 + 4 = 17$$

Here 1934 is the sum of the Revolution and 17 is the Prognostic figure. In the chapter on " Judgment from the Thirty-one Points," it will be seen that No. 17 denotes " Hope. Good or bad according to the sign." It indicates an epoch which will be highly beneficial or the reverse to the native. The Sum of the Nativity in the case of Napoleon Buonaparte is 25. In year 1795–1796, viz.: in his 27th year, he was appointed General-in-Chief of the Italian Army :—

$$1795$$
$$\underline{25}$$

$1820 = 1 + 8 + 2 + 0 = 11$

Prognostic XI. in the Major Points gives: Success by some remarkable and bold enterprises; obstacles are surmounted. In 1798 he undertook the Egyptian Campaign :—

$$1798$$
$$\underline{25}$$

$1823 = 1 + 8 + 2 + 3 = 14$

Point XIV. gives: Great perils; much need of initiative and of decision.

In May, 1804, he was proclaimed Emperor of France. As he was born in August of 1769, we must take the prognostic from the Revolutions of 1803 :—

$$1803$$
$$\underline{25}$$

$1828 = 1 + 8 + 2 + 8 = 19$

Point XIX. gives: Great fortune. Honours, glory, reputation. In 1815 he met with entire reversal of fortune, and his fall was then prognosticated :—

$$1815$$
$$\underline{25}$$

$1840 = 1 + 8 + 4 + 0 = 13$

Point XIII. gives: Ambitions and hopes deceived. This is the symbol of the Reaper, the destroyer.

Shelley's " Sum of Nativity " is 39. The year of his death was thus shown :—

$$1822$$
$$\underline{39}$$

$1861 = 1 + 8 + 6 + 1 = 16$

Point XVI. gives: Reversals. Danger of ruin. Catastrophes.

These examples will serve to show the method of procedure in regard to prognostics drawn from the Sum of the Nativity. A general prognostic of the whole life may be drawn from the key number when added to the year of birth, and extended, as in the examples above.

Some writers affirm that the age of a person added to the year when such age is attained, and extended, is sufficient for general prognostics. This is in experience oftentimes true. For example : In 1804, when Napoleon I. was declared Emperor, he was 35 years of age ; $1804 + 35 = 1839 = 1 + 8 + 3 + 9 = XXI.$ " High elevation, great honours, according to one's station." In 1815, the year of his downfall, he was 46 years of age. $1815 + 46 = 1861 = 1 + 8 + 6 + 1 = XVI.$ " Reversal, danger of ruin, catastrophes."

This method, to the extent to which it is reliable, has the advantage of simplicity, and can be applied without recourse to the key number of the Nativity.

CHAPTER XVI

The Eighth Circle

The foregoing methods of prognostication are used as auxiliaries to the following, which affords a more complete and certain method of forecasting events.

In addition to the Seven Planetary Circles treated of in the earlier part of this Manual, there is an Eighth Circle, called the "Circle of the Rosy Cross," and the "Hermetic Circle," from which prognostics are drawn as from a natal horoscope, when set out according to the rules appertaining to the Scale of the Revolution, which will now be given in detail.

The *Scale of the Revolution* is prepared somewhat after the manner of the Scale of Nativity, the only difference being that the key number must be added to the year under consideration (as previously to the year of birth) in order to get the Sum of the Revolution ; and further, the planetary positions are taken from the 8th Circle. Some take the Revolutional positions from the Circle of the Planet ruling the year under consideration, but experience shows that the 8th Circle is specially prepared for the yearly figures, and yields the most reliable prognostics. If we take the 85th year of Mr. Gladstone, whose figure of birth we already have, the process may be shown step by step.

I.—By the "Rising of the Signs" it will be seen that in the 85th year of life the ruling sign is found in the 1st House ; and that the sign which was on the ascendant in the nativity is rising again. Capricornus, therefore, will be the ruling sign for the year. It is technically called the *Processional Sign*, or the *Sign of Procession*. We must, therefore, set out a figure with Capricorn rising, and dispose the rest of the Signs in accordance therewith.

II.—The key-number of the nativity which was found to be 40, is added to the year 1893, as the 85th year of life takes its rise from 28th December (vulg. 29) 1893. Therefore :—

$$1893$$
$$40$$
—————
1933 = Sum of Revolution.

III.—We now proceed in the usual way to prepare the Scale of the Revolution, *as if for the birth of a person*, the key-number being 40.

N.B.—As the key-number contains the sign and the degree of birth, it is necessary to keep the same sign and degree in the Scale of Revolution as in that of the Nativity. If a figure may be taken from the Circle of the planet ruling the year of Revolution, then the process will be different, the sign and degree undergoing a change, together with the key-number. In this work, however, the 8th Circle only is consulted for the Revolution.

The elements required for this illustration are :—

Sum of Revolution.. ..	1933	=	10th house.
Surname	149	=	11th ,,
Second Christian Name..	60	=	12th ,,
First Christian Name ..	84	=	1st ,,
Degree	7	=	2nd ,,
Sign	10	=	3rd ,,
Year	1893	=	4th ,,

The elements which from year to year create the difference in the disposition of the planets are :—(1) The Sum of Revolution ; (2) The year ; (3) The processional rising of the signs. These produce an almost endless series of variations in the annual figures, as experiment would show.

THE HERMETIC CIRCLE.

No.	Point.	Planet.	Sign.
1	i.	..	..
2	ii.	☽	..
3	iii.	♀	..
4	iv.	♃	..
5	v.	♂	♈
6	vi.	☽	♉
7	vii.	☉	♊
8	viii.	♀	♋
9	ix.	♃	♌
10	x.	☿	♍
20	xi.	♂	..
3	xii.	☽	♎
40	xiii.	⚳	Reaper
50	xiv.	☉	♏
60	xv.	♄	♐
70	xvi.	♃	♑
80	xvii.	☿	..
90	xviii.	♀	♒
100	xix.	♃	♓
200	xx.	♄	..
300	xxi.	☉	..
400	xxii.	..	..
9	xxiii.	Royal Star	♌
5	xxiv.	♂	♈
6	xxv.	☿	♉
7	xxvi.	♃	♊
1	xxvii.	..	..
2	xxviii.	☽	..
3	xxix.	♀	..
4	xxx.	♃	..
5	xxxi.	☉	♈
6	xxxii.	☽	♉
7	xxxiii.	♂	♊
8	xxxiv.	♀	♋
9	xxxv.	♄	♌
10	xxxvi.	☉	♍
6	xxxvii.	Royal Star	♉
8	xxxviii.	☿	♋
9	xxix.	♃	♌
10	xl.	♀	♍
20-1	xli.	♂	..

No.	Point.	Planet.	Sign.
30–2	xlii.	☽	♎
40–3	xliii.	⚳	Reaper
50–4	xliv.	♂	♏
60–5	xlv.	☿	♐
70–6	xlvi.	♃	♑
80–7	xlvii.	☿	..
90–8	xlviii.	♀	♒
100–9	xlix.	♄	♓
200–10	l.	♄	..
90	li.	Royal Star	♒
30	lii.	♄	♎
50	liii.	☉	♏
60	liv.	☽	♐
1	lv.	†	Sword
2	lvi.	☽	..
3	lvii.	♀	..
4	lviii.	♃	..
5	lix.	♀	♈
6	lx.	♄	♉
7	lxi.	☉	♊
8	lxii.	☽	♋
9	lxiii.	♂	♌
10	lxiv.	☿	♍
50	lxv.	Royal Star	♏
70	lxvi.	♂	♑
90	lxvii.	☿	♒
100	lxviii.	♃	♓
20–1	lxix.	♂ Crowned	..
30–2	lxx.	♃	♎
40–3	lxxi.	⚳	Reaper
50–4	lxxii.	♀	♏
60–5	lxxiii.	♄	♐
70–6	lxxiv.	☉	♑
80–7	lxxv.	☿	..
90–8	lxxvi.	☽	♒
100–9	lxxvii.	♂	♓
200–10	lxxviii.	♄	..

Whenever a point occurs in the Scale of the figure which has no planet or sign against it in the Circle, the Point itself is to be marked in Roman figures in the House to which it rightly belongs. The interpretations of the different Points have already been given in a previous chapter (vide *Judgment by the Thirty-one Points*).

Now taking the elements afforded by the 85th year of Mr. Gladstone's horoscope, we may apply them to the 8th Circle, as follows :—

SCALE OF REVOLUTION.

x. 1933	10	♄
	9	♂ in ♌
	30	♃ in ♎
	3	Reaper
xi. 149	100	♂ in ♓
	40	Reaper
	9	R. ✱ ♌
xii. 60	60	☿ in ♐
i. 84	80	☿
	4	♃
ii. 7	7	☉ in ♊
iii. 10	10	☿ in ♍
iv. 1893	10	♄
	8	♀ in ♋
	90	♀ in ♒
	3	♀

N.B.—The Point of Departure is L, as for the Nativity, for the position of the Radical Sun is taken in the Scale, viz., ♑ 7°.

From this Scale we can erect the following :—

FIGURE OF REVOLUTION.

We do not need to look very minutely for the indications of an impending change in the career of the illustrious native. The return of the radical ruling sign Capricorn to the ascendant, with Mercury and Jupiter therein, as at the birth ; cardinal signs on angles, and the ruler of the figure in its fall in the 4th House, joined to a triple Venus, throwing rays from the 2nd and 7th Houses into the sign of its detriment, Aries ; and finally a ray from Mars in the 8th House to the tenth, where Libra the sign of its fall holds sway ; these are all indications of the change which followed in the spring of 1894. Venus, the ruler of the Revolutional 10th, is found twice *reflected*, and once *placed* in the 4th House in the sign of its " fall " ; and, furthermore, is afflicted by the conjunction of Saturn in Aries.

The *Point of Health* falls in the 12th House, being counted from Scorpio to Libra, i.e., from Saturn to Jupiter (*vide* General Rules). In this position we find Sagittarius with Mercury, the lord of the 6th therein ; a bad indication.

The *Point of Fortune* falls in the 11th House in Scorpio, where, together with two rays from Mars, from Pisces and Leo, we find the Reaper, which, while giving the support of friends, carries with it a menace to the fortunes ; for the Reaper destroys wherever he appears in a horoscope. Now observe that the prognostic for the year under consideration is XVI., thus :—

$$1893$$
$$40$$
_____

1933 $= 1 + 9 + 3 + 3 = $ XVI.

And this gives : CHANGE OR REVERSAL OF POSITION ; danger of ruin ; catastrophes.

Examples might be multiplied, but the above will be sufficient to show the use of the 8th Circle in the making of Annual Figures.

Now, if it be required to know at what time the threatened reversal of position would take place, note what planet signifies the position in the annual figure, and what planet is naturally opposed to it ; the position of this planet will indicate the time of the event, according to its sign. Thus : In the above figure Venus is the significator of the position (and we have seen how its position is wholly referred to the sign of its detriment) ; while Mars is the ruler of the 4th House, the opposite to the 10th. The planet Mars is found in Leo and in Pisces. Counting from Capricorn, which indicates the month of December-January, we first come to Pisces, which denotes the month of February-March, 1894, and it was in that month that the ex-Premier resigned his office. All other questions may be judged, in regard to time of event, in a similar manner. Thus from the position of Mercury, the ruler of the 6th House in Sagittarius and Virgo, and of Jupiter in Libra, we may judge of times of illness. Virgo corresponds to August-September, and Sagittarius to November-December, 1894.

CHAPTER XVII

General Examples.—No. I

For the purpose of illustrating more completely the scheme which has been set forth in these pages, it will be necessary to take some few examples. The first of these is the Horoscope of Percy Bysshe Shelley, the Lyric Poet, born 4th August, 1792, in the evening :—

P = 8 × 5 = 40	B = 2 × 6 = 12	S = 3 × 7 = 21
E = 5 × 4 = 20	Y = 1 × 5 = 5	H = 8 × 6 = 48
R = 2 × 3 = 6	S = 3 × 4 = 12	E = 5 × 5 = 25
C = 2 × 2 = 4	S = 3 × 3 = 9	L = 3 × 4 = 12
Y = 1 × 1 = 1	H = 8 × 2 = 16	L = 3 × 3 = 9
	E = 5 × 1 = 5	E = 5 × 2 = 10
		Y = 1 × 1 = 1
Total 71	Total 59	Total 126

The Sun on 4th August is found in the 12th degree of Leo, the 5th Sign. 7159126125 — 39.

The planet ruling the year 1792 is the Moon, therefore the key-number of the Nativity — 39 on the Circle of the Moon.

Referring to this Point in the Lunar Circle we find against it the symbol, "Moon in Leo." Turning to the Moon in Leo, in the chapter on the "Planets in the Twelve Signs," we read : "This is the astral signature of the Poet, of the man of Genius. The Moon, which gives imagination, joined to the Sun (Leo is the House of the Sun, the giver of Light) makes superior natures, those who possess true knowledge, omniscience."

Now, adding the key-number to the year of birth we get the "Sum of the Horoscope," thus :—

1792
39
‾‾‾‾
1831 — Sum of the Horoscope.

Hence we derive the Prognostic :—1 — 8 — 3 — 1 — XIII. (in the Thirty-one Points) : "Ambitions and hopes deceived." This is the Point of the Reaper, the destroyer. According to the Tarot, this Point further indicates,

In the Divine World : Creation and Transformation. In the Intellectual World : Ascension of the Spirit, exaltation of faculty. In the Physical World : Premature Death.

Tracing the Scale of the Nativity from the elements before us, we have as follows :—

x.	{	10	♂ in ♍
1831		8	♂ in ♋
		30	☉ in ♎
		1	Sword—Point lv.

126 x.	100	♀ in ♓
	20	♂ Crowned—Point lxix.
	6	♄ in ♑
xii. 59	50	☉ ♏ xiv.
	9	R ✶ ♌
i. 71	70	☿ in ♑
	1	Sword—Point lv.
ii. 12	10	♃ in ♍
	2	☿ in ♎
iii. 5	5	☉ in ♐
iv. 1792	10	♄
	7	☉ in ♊—vii.
	90	♀ in ♒—xviii.
	2	☽

The Point of Departure, due to the 2nd Decan of Leo, is **xxxvi.**

The figure of the Horoscope thus obtained is a very complicated one, and we leave the student to erect it from the Scale of Nativity which is given above; and we may pass at once to a consideration of the figure in the more important matter of the Astrological judgment.

Leo rises, with the Royal Star therein, a ray from Mercury in Capricorn in the 6th House, and the symbol of the Sword. The Royal Star of Leo denotes "the patronage of high personages," and celebrity. The *Sword* therein corresponding to Point LV. of the Hermetic Circle is a protection to the good and a menace to the wrong-doer. Also enterprises, which will be realized in spite of obstacles. In this case it denotes danger to life and honour (for it is also present in the 10th House). But let the Sign Leo give its testimony. When rising (see Chapter XIV.) it signifies that "affairs will necessitate short journeys. Some loss during such travels will occur. Harmful enterprises. Harm from friends in matters of money and property. (This was amply fulfilled in the native's life, owing chiefly to his own reckless generosity) Trouble through children. (Shelley was denied the custody of his children by Harriet, his first wife.) Family suffering. The position will be greatly benefited, or the reverse (this sign is hazardous in the question of position). A death will be profitable to the native (i.e., he gains by inheritance, or legacy). Serious losses by gaming or speculation, if indulged in. It will be necessary for the native to avoid yachting, boating, and bathing under dangerous circumstances, for there is some indication of drowning. The wife will be sick, or afflicted by troubles. The placing of the affections will create enmities in the native's life. Hidden enemies will seek to injure the position. Distrust of servants."

These prognostics are such as shed a great deal of true light upon the career under notice. Applied in general terms they afford a judgment from the Rising Sign, which is the more reliable because that sign has a radical and lasting influence over the life.

The honour and fame of the native was not, during his life-time, anything of which the most insignificant person need be jealous. Owing to his peculiar views of life, and his boldness in living close to those views, showing in every possible way the courage of his convictions, he necessarily attracted much criticism and enmity, while his name was something for M. Prudhomme and Mrs. Grundy to conjure with, when running a tirade against social reforms. This is amply shown in the Horoscope by a double ray from Mars (in Cancer in 12th, and in Virgo in 2nd) to the 10th House, where Taurus, the sign of its detriment, holds possession. To these is added a ray from the Sun in Libra, another debility; and the symbol of the Sword, a menace. The 11th House, however, is more fortunate; for therein we see a ray from Venus in Pisces; the symbol of Mars crowned; the Sun; and a ray from Saturn out of its own sign Capricorn; all converging in the fortunate Sign Gemini, ruler of the 3rd House, of intellect, and men of letters. Yet even here there is a danger, for Gemini is a " double " sign, and is capable of conferring a double nature upon those indicated thereby; and moreover the Sun and Saturn do not agree together. Hence, there was danger of duplicity and of distrust among the friends of the native, and dissensions of a lasting character.

The Point of Life is counted from Libra, the Moon at birth being past the full. The Moon is found in the 1st House past Libra, viz.: in Scorpio, and the Point, therefore, falls in the 1st House of the Horoscope, where we find the Sword and the Royal Star of Leo, together with a ray from Mercury in the 6th House. The latter is evil, and especially as it proceeds from a violent sign Capricorn; while the position of the Sun, ruler of the 1st House in its fall in Libra, does not encourage the prognostic with regard to length of days. But as the Point falls in the Ruling Sign, the Prognostic largely depends thereon, and we have seen that it denotes " danger of drowning." Counting to the Point of Death, viz.: from Moon in 4th to the 8th House — 4 signs; and then from Saturn in 6th to the same number, we come to the 10th House and the Sign Taurus, wherein we place the Point of Death. Here we find two evil rays from Mars (rendered evil by falling in Taurus), and a debilitated ray from the Sun in Libra, with, once more, the menace of the Sword. Observe, too, that the Sun sends its ray from the 3rd House, denoting short journeys, and Mars from Cancer in the 12th (dangers by sea), and the sign Virgo, wherein is the Constellation Argo—the Ship; a sign which is dangerous for nautical pursuits. But, the End of Life, signified by the 4th House, admits of no doubt in this matter. Therein we find the terribly evil sign Scorpio, with the Sun, Saturn, Venus, and the Moon; Venus throwing its ray from the 7th House, and the sign of Saturn, Aquarius. The Point of Death falling in Taurus, the significator is Venus and the enemy is Mars. These planets make their Conjunction in the 30th year (see Table of *Annual Conjunctions*, Chapter XIV.), and Mars in Cancer in the 12th denotes the month, June-July. The prognostic for the 30th year of life, which reaches to 1822, is as follows :—

$$1822$$
$$30$$

$$1852 = 1 + 8 + 5 + 2 = 16$$

The Sixteenth Point is " The Blasted Tower " : overthrow, ruin, catastrophe, accidents, falls, danger of the elements. While sailing unattended in the Bay of Spezzia on the afternoon of 8th July, 1822, the poet's boat was suddenly capsized by a storm, and he was drowned.

By the rising of the signs we obtain for the 30th year, the Processional Sign Capricorn ; but as the 30th year at the time of death was completed all but one month, we must take the sign for the 31st year and subtract therefrom the proportional rising for one month, viz. : 2½ degrees, which is at the rate of 30 degrees, or 1 Sign for a year. This brings the Sign Aquarius to the Ascendant, and as the 12th degree will come up on the 30th birthday, by subtracting 2½ degrees therefrom, we obtain Aquarius 9½ degree for July, 1822, corresponding to the Age of the Poet, 29 years 11 months.

Turning then to the prognostic for the rising of Aquarius, we find, among other things : " A very dangerous period. Physical dangers caused by oneself on water, or in relation to that element."

The above delineation will be sufficient, no doubt, to indicate by what means the presages of life and fortune may be drawn from the name of a person when treated according to the rules of the Kabalistic art. In this case we see how the key-number of the Nativity, when referred to the Planetary Circle of Birth, gives at once the key-note of the native's life ; the Moon in Leo ; Signature of the Poet, of the man of Genius. How, also, the Sum of the Horoscope indicates premature death, by the symbol of the Reaper, Point XIII., and how, taking the presages afforded by the rising of the signs, the planetary conjunctions, and the Sum of the Revolution, we gain an accurate knowledge of the facts of the native's life. But lest there should be any doubt as to these presages being a matter of *chance* (though we Astrologers do not know the word), the following Scale of the Revolution, for the 30th year, is subtended :—

It will be observed that the 30th Revolution takes its origin from 4th August, 1821, with Capricorn 12 degree, rising by Annual Procession.

SCALE OF REVOLUTION.

Point of Departure on 8th Circle.—Point xxxvi.

x.	10	☉ in ♍
1860	8	☿ in ♋
Sum of Revolution.	60	☿ in ♐
xi.	100	♄ in ♓
126	20	♂ Crowned
Surname.	6	☉ in ♑
xii.	50	☉ in ♏
59	9	R ♓ ♌
2nd Christian Name.		
i.	70	♃ in ♑
71	1	Sword
1st Christian Name.		
ii.	10	☿ in ♍
12	2	♃ in ♎
Degree.		
iii.	5	♄ in ♐
5		
Sign.		
iv.	10	♄
1821	8	♀ in ♋
Year.	20	♂
	1	Sceptre.

Here we find the Ruler of the figure, Saturn, posited in its fall in Aries in the 4th House ; in Pisces in the 3rd House ; and in Sagittarius in the 12th. All these are evil. The first position of Saturn in the Scale is that in Pisces. Turning to " Saturn in Pisces " in the Chapter on *Judgment by Position*, we find this prognostic : Danger of falling into water. Accidental or voluntary drowning.

Observe also that Saturn is posited in the 3rd House, that of short journeys, and in a watery sign ; being also repeated in the 12th House—wherein it is especially evil—and throwing a malefic ray into the 3rd House.

Calculating the Points of *Death* and of *Voyages*, according to the rules already laid down in a previous chapter, we find that both of these points fall in the 4th House, in the violent sign Aries, in conjunction with Saturn and Mars, and a ray from Venus in Cancer (fateful sign of the ocean), rendered malefic by falling into Aries, the sign of its debility. The rulers of the year, Mars and Venus (see Table of Annual Conjunctions) are here concerned in the presage of death.

$$\begin{array}{r} 1821 \\ 39 \\ \hline \end{array}$$

$1860 = 1 + 8 + 6 + 0 = $ XV., which gives : *Predestination, fatality, the unforeseen.* When, therefore, the sign Aquarius came up to the 1st House by procession, the predestined event so clearly indicated herein came to pass. The student will notice that the sign of the Nativity, Leo, passed into the 8th House (of Death) at the outset of the 30th year of life.

CHAPTER XVIII

GENERAL EXAMPLES.—No. II

MARIE-FRANÇOIS-SADI CARNOT, born 11th August, 1837, increasing Moon, in the year of Jupiter; evening horoscope; Sun in Leo 19.

M 4 × 5 = 20	F 8 × 8 = 64	S 3 × 4 = 12	C 2 × 6 = 12
A 1 × 4 = 4	R 2 × 7 = 14	A 1 × 3 = 3	A 1 × 5 = 5
R 2 × 3 = 6	A 1 × 6 = 6	D 4 × 2 = 8	R 2 × 4 = 8
I 1 × 2 = 2	N 5 × 5 = 25	I 1 × 1 = 1	N 5 × 3 = 15
E 5 × 1 = 5	Ç 2 × 4 = 8		O 7 × 2 = 14
	O 7 × 3 = 21		T 4 × 1 = 4
	I 1 × 2 = 2		
	S 3 × 1 = 3		
Total 37	Total 143	Total 24	Total 58

371432458195 — **52** key-number, Circle of Jupiter. Point of Departure XXXVI.

Point 52 in the Circle of Jupiter gives: Moon in Libra, whence the following characteristics are drawn: Romanesque and poetic imagination. Good conscience, rectitude, integrity. *Popularity acquired at the Bar, or in the administration of justice.*

1837 year of birth.
  35 key-number of Nativity.

1889 — Sum of Horoscope.

SCALE OF NATIVITY.

x. 1889	10	♀ in ♍	
	8	♀ in ♋	
	80	☿	
	9	♃ in ♓	
xi. 58	50	☉ in ♏	
	8	☿ in ♋	
xii. 24	20	♂ Crowned	
	4	♃ in ♏	
i. 143	100	♄ in ♓	
	40	Point xiii. ♪ Reaper.	
	3	♀	
ii. 37	30	☿ in ♎	
	7	☿	
iii. 19	10	♄	
	9	☽ in ♌	
iv. 5	5	☿ in ♐	
v. 1837	10	♄	
	8	♀ in ♋. viii.	
	30	☽ in ♎. xii.	
	7	♂ in ♊	

The figure being constructed from the above Scale, one sees immediately certain signs of excellent fortune, and certain others of the most inimical character. The House of Life, the 1st House, contains the Reaper, Point XIII., symbol of untimely death; with a ray from Saturn in Pisces from the 8th House, and Saturn ruling the 6th (Perils). The Point of Life, when calculated, falls in the 6th House in the sign Capricorn, and that of Death falls in the 1st House in Leo; the Moon, ruler of the 12th (secret enemies) sends a ray from the 1st House to the 3rd (short journeys) and observe that it is in a *male* sign and in Leo, which rules Italy. Danger during short journeys, therefore, is plainly imminent. But lest there be any doubt in the matter, observe the 3rd House itself. It contains Mercury, Saturn, and Moon in the sign Libra, and the Moon in Libra is derived from the XIIth Point of the Circle of birth. Against it we read: Reversal; danger of a violent or public death. It is the 12th Arcanum of the Tarot, the Reversed Triangle, signifying: Catastrophe.

And now observe the Moon in the 3rd House sends a ray (vitiated by a conjunction of Saturn) into the 5th House (galas, festivals, etc.), where it joins Mercury in Sagittarius, Saturn, a ray from Mars in Gemini in the 11th House, and one from Venus in Cancer in the 12th.

The Point of Peril falls in the 10th House, showing dangers while in the commission of public duties. Here again Mercury is found, as in the 12th (secret enemies), the 3rd (journeys), and the 5th (festivals), while from the latter he throws a ray into the violent and secret sign Scorpio, in the 4th House. It is this planet which, joining the Sun, ruler of the figure, in the Annual Conjunction of the 57th year of life, gives the presage of death.

The Point of Enemies is in the 9th House, in the violent sign Aries, afflicting the Point of Life in 6th House in Capricorn; and in square to the 12th House. In the 57th year this sign Aries comes up to the Ascendant, while the ruling sign passes into the 5th House. Consequently, enemies are stirred up, and when the following sign Taurus came up to the 1st House, it brought with it the " Point of Perils "; and this happened some few months previous to the Death. The " Point of Death," which falls in Leo, was in the 5th House when the " Point of Perils " was in the 1st House. The presage drawn from the preceding birthday, or annual revolution, would be from the rising of the sign Aries, and the passage of the ruling sign into the 5th House. The rising of Aries shows " danger of wounds "; and " harmful journeys "; while the ruling sign in the 5th House shows " Danger of treachery," among other things. These, however, are only general prognostics and gain their value from the special positions referred to in the Horoscope before us. By referring the age of the subject, viz.: 57 years, to the year of his death, 1894, we get: $1894 + 57 = 1951 = 1 + 9 + 5 + 1 = XVI.$ Reversals; danger of ruin; catastrophe!

CHAPTER XIX

GENERAL EXAMPLES.—No. III

NAPOLEONE BUONAPARTE,[1] born 15th August, 1769, morning; Moon increasing; Sun in Leo 23 degrees. Circle Venus.

N	5 × 9 = 45		B	2 × 10 = 20		
A	1 × 8 = 8		U	6 × 9 = 54		
P	8 × 7 = 56		O	7 × 8 = 56		
O	7 × 6 = 42		N	5 × 7 = 35		
L	3 × 5 = 15		A	1 × 6 = 6		
E	5 × 4 = 20		P	8 × 5 = 40		
O	7 × 3 = 21		A	1 × 4 = 4		
N	5 × 2 = 10		R	2 × 3 = 6		
E	5 × 1 = 5		T	4 × 2 = 8		
			E	5 × 1 = 5		

Total 222 Total 234

222234235 = 25♀. Key-number.
1769 + 25 = 1794. Sum of Horoscope.

1 + 7 + 9 + 4 = xxi. Prognostic: "High positions. Considerable honours, according to the sphere of life." *This is the symbol of the highest fortune to which man may aspire! This Supreme Talisman, the "Crown," indicates that all obstacles will be cleared from the path of the native, and his achievements be limited only by his will.*

The Point of Departure for this horoscope, afforded by the Sun in the third Decan of Leo, is XL. on the Circle of Venus, which planet rules the year of birth.

SCALE OF NATIVITY.

x.	⎰	10	Mercury in Virgo.
1794	⎱	7	Mercury.
		90	Roy. ✳ of Aquarius. Pt. lv.
		4	Jupiter.
xi.	⎰	200	Saturn.
234	⎱	30	Moon in Libra. Pt. xii.
		4	Jupiter.
xii.	⎰	200	Saturn
222	⎱	20	Mars Crowned.
		2	Sun in Libra.
i.	⎰	20	Mars. Point xi.
23	⎱	3	Venus.
ii.	⎱	5	Mercury in Aries.
5	⎰		

[1] This is the Corsican spelling.

		10	Saturn in Virgo.
iii.		7	Mercury.
1769		60	Saturn in Sagittarius.
		9	Mars in Leo.

This figure is so remarkable, that, for the better and more lucid interpretation of its singular presages, it is here reproduced in horoscopical form.

HOROSCOPE OF NAPOLEON I.

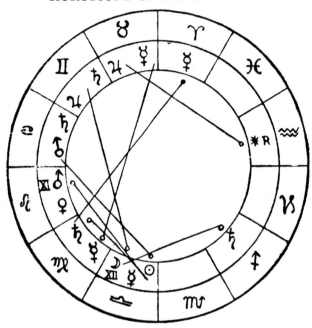

The key-number of the Nativity joins with all other testimonies to presage, high ambitions ; conquests ; and attainment. The symbol of Point XXV. is a man on horseback, sceptre in hand, fully armed. It denotes high offices ; strife, which conquers its way to the Sun ; power that is acquired by strife.

The Decan under which birth takes place denotes : " High elevation by good fortune ; inflexible character ; obstinate in purpose ; adventurous spirit ; martial and governmental capacity."

But observe the Ruler of the Nativity, in its *fall*, the sign Libra, in square to Mars and Saturn in the sign Cancer in the 12th House. Do we not see here the presage of an eventual fall, made worse by reason of the heights attained ? See Mars in the 1st House, in the Regal Sign Leo, and associated with the XIth Point: " Success by some bold enterprises. Obstacles surmounted." Jupiter and Mercury in the 10th House, with a ray from the Royal Star of Aquarius (Point LI.) denoting, " High position and dignity, by good fortune."

But on the other hand, what evils threaten the illustrious native! The *Point of Life*—calculated from Aries to the Moon, according to rule—falls in the 6th House ; and Saturn, its ruler, is in the 12th

House, the place of *exile and imprisonment,* and in Cancer its greatest debility.

The *Point of Death* is in Scorpio in the 4th House ; while Mars, its ruler, is joined to Saturn in the 12th again.   There, also, we see a ray from the Lord of the Horoscope, in the sign of its *fall,* Libra.

The *Point of Enemies* falls in the 9th House, in the sign Aries (England's ruler), opposite to the ruler of the Horoscope, the sign of eventual defeat.   Turning now to the significators, Mars and Saturn, in the 12th House, we find one to produce " Bold enterprises," and the other, " Danger to the position."

Several points of interest have already been noticed in connexion with the prognostics from the Annual " Sum of the Revolution," and there are many others which the ingenious reader will discover for himself ; suffice it in this instance to remark, in conclusion, that the lord of the 6th, Saturn, in the 12th House in Cancer, joined to Mars and afflicting the Sun and Moon in Libra, indicates death from disease during exile, such disease being in the part ruled by Cancer ; and it is well known that Napoleon died of *Cancer in the Stomach* on the 5th May, 1821, at St. Helena.   The luminous presages of this horoscope are the more wonderful from the fact that, in all cases, whether for pauper or prince, the same rules and methods are followed, both in construction and interpretation of the horoscope.

The elements for the Downfall of Napoleon in June, 1815, are as follows :—46th year of life begins 15th August, 1814 ; Sum of Horoscope — 1839 ; annual conjunction, Sun and Saturn ; rising sign, Taurus.

SCALE OF REVOLUTION.

Sum of Revolution	1839
Surname	234
Forename	222
Degree	23
Sign	5
Year	1814

The Point of Departure is XL.   Reference to the Eighth Circle affords the following extended scale of the Revolution :—

x. 1839	10	♀ in ♍
	8	♀ in ♒
	30	♄ in ♎
	9	♂ in ♌
xi. 234	200	♄
	30	☽ in ♎
	4	♃
xii. 222	200	♄
	20	♂ Crowned.
	2	♃ in ♎
i. 23	20	♂
	3	♀
ii. 5	5	☉ in ♈
iii. 1814	10	☉ in ♍
	8	☿ in ♋
	10	♀ in ♍
	4	♂ in ♎

A figure set out from this Scale shows the following points :—
The sign of the nativity passes into the 4th House ; the 7th House, that of *enemies*, is exalted in the 10th of the Revolution. These positions become augmented in their evil import when, later in this year of the Emperor's life, the 2nd Decan of Gemini comes to the ascendant, and the ruling sign passes into the 3rd House.

The annual conjunction of Saturn and Sun for the 46th year of life confirms the radical evil import of the nativity, wherein the Sun, ruler of the figure, is depressed in the sign of its fall, Libra ; and Saturn in the 12th, conjoined to Mars, and ruling the 7th (enemies), afflicts the Sun by a square aspect. In the Revolutional figure Saturn and the Sun are conjoined in the 12th, in opposition to the Moon and Saturn in the 6th.

The Point of Fortune falls in the 6th House, with Saturn, Moon, and Jupiter. Venus, the ruler of the figure, is also ruler of the 6th, and is in its debility in the sign Virgo ; thus the Point of Fortune comes to be badly placed both by House and Sign ; the 6th House, is at all times evil, and debilitates the planets which may fall therein, charging them with an influence of a contrary and discordant nature ; thus leading to strifes, to losses, and to physical ills.

Now observe that, when, two months before his 46th birthday, Napoleon was defeated at Waterloo, the sign Gemini had risen to the Ascendant, and the Ruling Sign of the Nativity (Leo) had passed into the 3rd House.

Gemini rising denotes : "Danger of a fall. Position is insecure. Danger of wounds."

The ruling sign passing into the 3rd House denotes : "Year of travel, more or less changes of residence and position. Menace of lasting hatreds and hidden ills. Disgrace through superiors. Loss of wealth and of friends. Envy and malignity. Sorry position."

The year 1815 was destined to be a fateful one to the Emperor, for the key-number added to it gives a sum of 1840 — Point XIII. The Reaper. "Ambitions and hopes deceived." The 46th year of life, when referred to the year in which it was attained, gives $1815 + 46 = 1861 = 1 + 8 + 6 + 1 =$ Point XVI. The Blasted Tower. "Reversal ; danger of ruin ; catastrophe."

The foregoing examples of Horoscopes calculated on the plan of the Kabalistic art will be sufficient to indicate the method to be followed in all other instances ; and I doubt not that the reader will find fresh illustrations of the singular value of this system of prognostication in his own nativity, and in others which his curiosity may suggest for experiment.

GENERAL EXAMPLES.—No. IV.

SOPHIA HICKMAN.

THE missing lady-doctor who mysteriously disappeared from the Royal Free Hospital on August 15, 1903, was born at Sydendam, Kent, on the 22nd June, 1874, in the afternoon. The Sun is in the first degree of Cancer. The "number of the name" is thus derived:—

S 3 × 6 = 18	F 8 × 7 = 56	H 8 × 7 = 56
O 7 × 5 = 35	R 2 × 6 = 12	I 1 × 6 = 6
P 8 × 4 = 32	A 1 × 5 = 5	C 2 × 5 = 10
H 8 × 3 = 24	N 5 × 4 = 20	K 2 × 4 = 8
I 1 × 2 = 2	C 2 × 3 = 6	M 4 × 3 = 12
A 1 × 1 = 1	E 5 × 2 = 10	A 1 × 2 = 2
	S 3 × 1 = 3	N 5 × 1 = 5
112	112	99

Key-number = 1121129941 = 31
Year   1874

Sum of Horoscope =   1905 = XV. Typhon.

Presage: Mystery, the unknown, the unexpected, fatality. (See Tarot keys in the following chapter.)

The following is the Scale of the Horoscope, from which the reader by the aid of the planetary Cycle will be able to erect the figure.

The year 1874 is under the Cycle of the Moon, and the 1st decan of Cancer gives the Point of Departure, 36.

SCALE OF HOROSCOPE.

Xth	House — 1905 = 10–9–5.
XIth	,, 99 = 90–9.
XIIth	,, 112 = 100–10–2.
Ist	,, 112 = 100–10–2.
IInd	,, 1 = 1.
IIIrd	,, 4 = 4.
IVth	,, 1874 = 10–8–70–4.

Miss Hickman entered her 30th year in June, 1903, and the Kabalism is significant:—

Year 1903
Age   30

1933

Then 1 + 9 + 3 + 3 = XVI.—" The Blasted Tower."

REVOLUTIONAL FIGURE.

Miss Sophia Hickman entered her 30th year in June, 1903, and the rising sign was then Sagittarius, which is evil for persons born under Cancer, as will be seen in Chapter XV. under the head of " The Processional Rising of the Signs."

The natal sign Cancer enters the 8th House in the 30th year of life and Sagittarius rises. Now the first decan of Sagittarius rising shows " troubles in connection with marriage." The planetary conjunction is Mars and Venus : " troubles in love affairs, passionate impulses." The ruling Sign in the 8th House also shows " injurious love affairs."

THE REVOLUTION FOR 1903

shows the following Scale, which is extracted from the 8th Circle, or Circle of the Rosy Cross :—

Sum of Horoscope ..	..	..	..	..	..	1934
Surname ..	..	..	..	..	..	99
Christian Names } ..	..	..	..	..	..	112
..	..	..	..	..	..	112
Degree ..	..	..	..	..	..	1
Sign ..	..	..	..	..	..	9
Year ..	..	..	..	..	..	1903

On erecting this figure it will be seen that the year is remarkable for the frequent recurrence of the ☽ in ♎ under the Major Point XII.

This point is rendered (Chapter XIII.) " Reversal of position, culpability, chastisement, danger of a violent death, either enforced or voluntary, catastrophe."

A careful reading of this horoscope will prove to be illuminative of much that still remains a mystery to all but the searcher of mysteries, than which none is greater than the veritable science of Sound and Number.

When a planet does not appear at all in a horoscope it is said to be *in obscuration.* In this horoscope we find Mercury (the intellect) in obscuration, showing a tendency to dementia.

GENERAL EXAMPLES.—No. **V.**

CECIL RHODES.

THE " Colossus " and founder of the British South African Empire was born on the 6th July, 1853, at 7 p.m.

The calculation is as follows :—

C 2 × 5 = 10	R 2 × 6 = 12
E 5 × 4 = 20	H 8 × 5 = 40
C 2 × 3 = 6	O 7 × 4 = 28
I 1 × 2 = 2	D 4 × 3 = 12
L 3 × 1 = 3	E 5 × 2 = 10
	S 3 × 1 = 3
――	――
41	105

The ☉ is in Cancer 15 degrees. Key-number = 41105415 = 21, *The Crown.*

Presage : This is the symbol of the highest elevation to which man can aspire. The supreme Talisman of fortune, this Crown denotes that every obstacle will be cleared from your path and that the ascension of destiny has no limits save those of your own will !

Sum of Horoscope 1853

21

―――――

1874 = XX.

This Point denotes " The Awakening." It shows " unexpected elevation," and " the revelation of genius."

SCALE OF HOROSCOPE.

X—Sum of Horoscope   ..   ..   ..   1874 = 10, 8, 70, 4.
XI—Surname   ..   ..   105 = 100, 5.
XII—Christian Name   ..   ..   ..   41 = 40, 1.
I—Degree   ..   ..   15 = 10, 5.
II—Sign   ..   ..   4 = 4.
III—Year   ..   ..   1853 = 10, 8, 50, 3.

Point of Departure, XL.—Circle.

The reader who has carefully digested the principles of Kabalistic Astrology will at once see in this horoscope the elements of a singular fortune.   In the 10th House, or House of Honours, we find the rays of the Sun and Moon converging with Venus and Mars ; the chief point being Mars in its own sign with Point V.—which is "The Master of Secrets "—the secret power of the human will.

The rising sign Cancer shows "voyages, marine traffic, publicity, good fortune, happiness, supremacy."   I should doubt if Cecil Rhodes ever knew what happiness really is ; but for the rest, it is faithful presage.   The second decan of Cancer gives "favourable chances of acquiring wealth," and the ray of the Moon to its own sign and that of Jupiter from its own sign (Sagittarius), together with the actual position of Jupiter in the 2nd House, are sure indications that all such chances would be taken advantage of.

On the side of friends (the 11th House) the horoscope is weak, for Mars' ray into Taurus, and Venus its ruler being in Virgo, are both indications adverse to the forming of beneficial friendships.   It may safely be said that the friends of Cecil Rhodes "meant well " but did badly for him.

In 1902 Cecil Rhodes was 49 years of age and he died that year; 1902 +49 = 1951 = XVI. This is the worst of all the Points: " The Blasted Tower "

GENERAL EXAMPLES.—No. VI.

JOSEPH CHAMBERLAIN.

THE late Colonial Secretary was born at Highbury, London, N., in the morning of the 8th July, 1836. The year is ruled by Venus, and the Sun is in the 17th of Cancer.

J $1 \times 6 =$ 6	C $2 \times 11 =$ 22	
O $7 \times 5 =$ 35	H $8 \times 10 =$ 80	
S $3 \times 4 =$ 12	A $1 \times 9 =$ 9	
E $5 \times 3 =$ 15	M $4 \times 8 =$ 32	
P $8 \times 2 =$ 16	B $2 \times 7 =$ 14	
H $8 \times 1 =$ 8	E $5 \times 6 =$ 30	
	R $2 \times 5 =$ 10	
	L $3 \times 4 =$ 12	
	A $1 \times 3 =$ 3	
	I $1 \times 2 =$ 2	
	N $5 \times 1 =$ 5	
——— 92	——— 219	

Key-number = 92219174 = 35.
Year of birth   1836
Key-number   35

Sum of Horoscope 1871 = XVII.

Presage : " The Mage's Star "—illumination, hope. This star has a special signification of an exceptional advent, and wherever seen gives hope of a new order of things, a particular dispensation. Seldom is one born under it who has not a particular mission to fulfil.

SCALE OF HOROSCOPE.

X.	Sum of Horoscope..	..	..	1871 = 10, 8, 70, 1.
XI.	Surname ..	..	..	..	219 = 200, 10, 9.
XII.	Christian name	..	..	..	92 = 90, 2.
I.	Degree ..	..	..	..	17 = 10, 7.
II.	Sign ..	..	..	..	4 = 4.
III.	Year ..	..	..	..	1836 = 10, 8, 30, 6.

Circle of Venus.   Point of Departure XI.

This horoscope is in some respects not unlike that of Cecil Rhodes. The 2nd decan of Cancer rises in each case, the Sun is in the 7th House in Capricorn, and Jupiter (the Star of Good Fortune) holds the 2nd House. But it is yet more fortunate than that of the Cape Premier.   Mars Crowned holds the position of greatest elevation in its own sign Aries, and it indicates success in strife; a reputation won at a hazard ; great fortune ; reputation ; honours by merit.   Saturn's influence coming from Aquarius is not by any means evil, but falling into Aries it becomes vitiated and the reputation will not be free from a suspicious tarnish. Mercury in Virgo throws a ray to the 10th House, denoting reputation gained by polemics ; a faculty for argument ; mathematical ability ; alertness and much knowledge of affairs relating to (Virgo) merchandise, trade, shipping, food, commodities, etc.

THE HOROSCOPE.

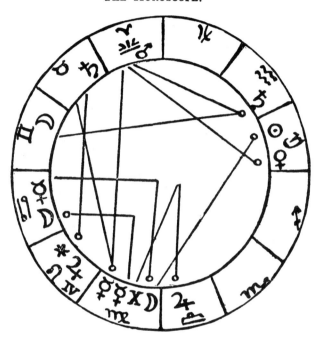

The Moon rising and associated with Mercury shows a restless, busy and alert mind ; popularity.   Jupiter with the *Royal Star of Leo* in the 2nd House gives financial success ; wealth ; favour of persons in authority ; celebrity and success in life.   The key-note of the horoscope is ambitious strife.

The year 1903 is one of the most successful of all those which are destined to contribute to Mr. Chamberlain's ambitious successes.   Added to the key-number 35, the year 1903 gives the Sum of the Horoscope XXI., *the Crown of the Magi*.   Also the age is 67 years in 1903, which, added together, gives the Kabalism 1970 = XVII., which is the *Star of the Magi*.   If the highest point of honour be not then obtained there are dangers and reversals to follow in 1904, when the presage is adverse in many ways.

CHAPTER XX

POLITICAL HOROSCOPES

I. THE BOER WAR.

THE following illustrations are intended to show how Kabalistic Astrology may be applied to general political forecasts and State affairs. The Boer War was declared on the 10th of October, 1899. The horoscope for England is taken from the preceding conjunction of the Sun and Moon, which occurred on the 4th October, 1899, being the year of the Sun; and the Sun on that date in the 12th degree of Libra. The contesting forces were represented by the Transvaal Republic and Great Britain. The enumeration of these names and the presage, derived from them will clearly show the fortunes of each as regards this war.

$$
\begin{array}{ll}
\text{G } 3 \times 5 = 15 \qquad & \text{B } 2 \times 7 = 14 \\
\text{R } 2 \times 4 = 8 & \text{R } 2 \times 6 = 12 \\
\text{E } 5 \times 3 = 15 & \text{I } 1 \times 5 = 5 \\
\text{A } 1 \times 2 = 2 & \text{T } 4 \times 4 = 16 \\
\text{T } 4 \times 1 = 4 & \text{A } 1 \times 3 = 3 \\
& \text{I } 1 \times 2 = 2 \\
& \text{N } 5 \times 1 = 5 \\
\hline
44 & 57
\end{array}
$$

☉ in 12 degrees of 7th Sign =
Key-number 4457127 = 30
Year 1899

Sum of Horoscope 1929 = XXI.

Presage : " The Crown of the Magi " : The Supreme Talisman of Fortune ! A most fortunate presage of the destiny of Great Britain, so far as the issues of any enterprise begun under the influence of this New Moon are concerned. The following is the

SCALE OF THE HOROSCOPE.

10th House—	1929	= 10,9,20,9.
11th ,,	57	= 50,7.
12th ,,	44	= 40,4.
1st ,,	12	= 10,2.
2nd ,,	7	= 7.
3rd ,,	1899	= 10,8,90,9.

Point of Departure LXIV.

X.	10	☿	in ♍	in the	12th House.
	9	♂	in ♓	,, ,,	6th ,,
	20	♂		,, ,,	10th ,,
	9	*	in ♌	,, ,,	11th ,,
XI.	50	♀	in ♏	,, ,,	2nd ,,
	7	☿		,, ,,	11th ,,
XII.	40	⚳		,, ,,	12th ,,
	4	☉	in ♏	,, ,,	2nd ,,
I.	10	♄		,, ,,	1st ,,
	2	☽		,, ,,	1st ,,
II.	7	☉	in ♊	,, ,,	9th ,,
III.	10	♃	in ♍	,, ,,	12th ,,
	8	♃	,, ♋	,, ,,	10th ,,
	90	♃	,, ♒	,, ,,	5th ,,
	9	☿	,, ♓	,, ,,	6th ,,

Here we find Mars and Jupiter in the 10th House, showing honours and success, and powerful allies. But there are rays from Mercury and Mars in opposition to one another, showing political strife and perfidy of dependents; while the ray from the Royal Star of Leo gives alliances of the most powerful nature and promises success. In the ascendant we find Saturn and the Moon, denoting privations of the people; and in the 2nd House, Venus, Sun and a ray from the Sun in Gemini in the 9th House, showing a difficult state of finance and that associated with foreign lands (☉ in 9th House).

THE TRANSVAAL REPUBLIC.

Gives the key-number 26, sum of the horoscope XVII.—Hope: true or false according to the positions of the planets in the horoscope. The horoscope is in many respects similar, starting as it does from the same point. But when once the name of the Republic begins to operate in the Scale of the Horoscope, there is a change, and we find the ☉ in the 7th House in Aries (the ruling Sign of England!), throwing a ray to the 10th House, and denoting powerful political enmity. The 10th House contains Mars and Mercury only, with opposing rays of the same planets from the 12th and 6th Houses. Where is the ray of the Royal Star of the Lion? Nowhere. Where is Jupiter? Nowhere, except throwing a vitiated ray into the 12th House from the 6th where it is conjoined with Mars.

What was the presage? *Hope*! Hope, with no promise of success.

Contrast this with the Presage for England: *The Crown*, with indubitable promise of success. It is enough, the mystery of Numbers is no longer a mystery but a revelation!

THE PASSING OF QUEEN VICTORIA.

This event, which took place in the midst of a period of severe British reversals in South Africa, was fraught with the most tragic of influences. It was indeed an example of the irony of Fate that one so wise and prudent, under whose beneficent reign England had prospered in all its many and great enterprises, should be called hence at a period of darkest gloom. But so it was, and the horoscope for the New Moon of the 20th January, 1901, which preceded the sad event by only two days, is especially significant of the national bereavement.

The Sun was in the 30th degree of Capricornus, which gives the Point of Departure LXXVIII. in the Circle of Mercury.

The name Victoria, when extended Kabalistically after the manner already shown, gives the value of 124, to which we add the 30th degree of the 10th Sign, and obtain :—

The key-number—1243010 = 11
Year 1901

—————

Sum of Horoscope 1912 = XIII.

Presage : Point XIII—" The Reaping Skeleton " i.e., Death.

Let the reader peruse the interpretation of the Arcanum in the *Tarot,* and also in the Judgment of the 31 Points in Chapter XIII, and he will find conviction of truth.

It is a presage of transformation, ambitions and hopes deceived, destruction, undoing and death. Rightly indeed does the oracular sentence fall, true to the incident of the day and hour : " Let the subject raise his mind above earthly things, for the disappointment of his hopes gives menace of a shortened life."

It may be urged that the coincidence is fortuitous. But a little study will show the vanity of the argument, for the only other years in Queen Victoria's life when the key-number was 11 were 1882, 1863, 1844 and 1823, when the lunation fell in Capricorn 30 on the 20th January ; and none of these years when added to the key-number yield the Sum of the Horoscope XIII, from which this fatal presage can be drawn.

This concludes my exposition of the art of Kabalistic Astrology. The examples adduced in illustration of the principles of this art are not selected on account of their singular agreement with those principles, but are taken as typical horoscopes of general interest. The same remarkable conformity is shown in scores of horoscopes drawn by me for private and inconspicuous persons, and although the construction of the " Circles " reveals a certain orderly disposition of the factors employed, yet it must ever remain a profound mystery as to how the originator of this ingenious system of prescience discovered the correspondence of horoscopical relations with name values and birthdays. Equally inexplicable is the marvellous Egyptian *Tarot* from the Golden Book of Hermes which constitutes the basis of this system of numerical interpretation. We can only take the facts as we find them, and admit in the face of so much evidence that " There are more things in Heaven and earth than are dreamed of in our philosophy."

CHAPTER XXI

The Tarot

An exposition of the XXII. Major Keys of the *Tarot* are added to the text of this work, and they will be found of singular use in the interpretation of Horoscopes, whether in reference to the Sum of a Horoscope, of a Revolutional figure, or of a Point falling within the Planetary Circle of birth. For a further exposition of their Kabalistic import, I must refer the reader to the works of Eliphas Levi, to the *Kabala Denudata* of S. Macgregor Mathers, and the *Sepher Yetzirah* (Book of Transformations) of Wynn Westcott. I have here reproduced only so much of the significations of the XXII. keys as may be useful in connection with the subject-matter of this Manual.

The Twenty-two Major Points.

Point I.—*The Magician.*

In the *Divine World* this Point represents the *Absolute Being,* who contains, and from whom enamates, all possible things.

In the *Intellectual World* it represents *Unity,* the principal and synthesis of numbers ; and *Will,* the principles of *Actions.*

In the *Physical World* it represents man as a relative being, a synthesis of the manifestations of life, called upon to raise himself by an eternal expansion into the concentric spheres of the Absolute.

In the *Horoscope* it indicates that a strong will and belief in himself, controlled by reason and a love of justice, will lead the native to his goal in life, and preserve him from all dangers by the way. In a lower sense it indicates the approach of mysterious events.

Point II.—*The Door of the Hidden Sanctuary.*

In the *Divine World* this Point symbolizes the consciousness of the Absolute Being, who sees and possesses the three terms of all manifestation, i.e., the past, present, and future.

In the *Intellectual World* it symbolizes the Binary, the reflection of the Unity ; science, perception of visible and invisible things.

In the *Physical World* the Woman, image of the Man, uniting herself to him for the accomplishment of the same destiny.

In the *Horoscope* it indicates that the Mind perceives through the eyes of the will. God said : " Let there be light," and light inundated the infinitudes. Man, image of God, should say : " Let truth be manifest that Good may prevail, and if the man possess a forceful will, truth will be manifest unto him, and he will attain to the Good that he seeks.

Let him knock and the door will be opened to him ; but let him study well the way by which he must enter.

Let him turn his face towards the Sun of Righteousness, and the Knowledge of Truth will be given to him. Let him keep silence with regard to his purposes that they may not be open to vulgar disputation.

Point III.—*Isis Urania.*

In the *Divine World* this Point symbolizes *Supreme Power*, balanced by a perpetually active intelligence, and by absolute wisdom.

In the *Intellectual World* : The universal fecundity of all forms of being.

In the *Physical World* : Nature in travail, the germination of acts which proceed from the will.

In the *Horoscope* : To will what is possible is to have created it ; to will the impossible is to give oneself over to destruction.

Let the native hope for success in his undertakings if he knows how to unite a fruitful activity to rectitude of mind, which fructifies all works.

Point IV.—*The Stone Cube.*

In the *Divine World* : The perpetual and successional realization of the Virtues contained in the Absolute Being.

In the *Intellectual World* : The realization of the ideas of dependent being by the fourfold working of the spirit : Affirmation, Negation, Discussion, and Solution.

In the *Physical World* : The realization of acts directed by true knowledge, right will, and good work.

In the *Horoscope* : Nothing can resist the steadfast will, based upon the consciousness of Truth and Justice. To wish for that which is right and true, and to fight for its realization, is more than a right : it is a duty. The man who triumphs in this struggle has only accomplished his mission. He who fails has acquired immortality. The realization of a man's hopes depends upon one more powerful than he ; let him, therefore, strive to know that One, and to gain help therefrom.

Point V.—*The Master of the Secrets.*

In the *Divine World* : Universal law ; the regulator of the infinite manifestations of being in the one substance.

In the *Intellectual World* : Religion, the connection between the Absolute and Relative Beings, between the Infinite and the Finite.

In the *Physical World* : Inspiration communicated by the vibrations of the Astral Fluid ; the trial of man through liberty of Action within the unpassable circle of Universal law.

In the *Horoscope* : If one would know whether a man be happy or unhappy, find out what use he has made of his Will, for " Every man recreates himself in his works." The future is under the influence of a good or evil Genius.

If a man retire into the silence and solitude of his heart, an inward voice will speak to him ; let Conscience make answer.

Point VI.—*The Two Ways.*

In the *Divine World* : Knowledge of Good and Evil.

In the *Intellectual World* : The equilibrium of Necessity and Liberty ; of Duty and Right.

In the *Physical World* : The antagonism of natural forces, the binding of effects to their causes.

In the *Horoscope* : For the majority of men, vice has more attractions than the austere beauty of virtue.

Let one take care of his resolutions, for obstacles bar the way to happiness ; contrary forces surround him, and his will fluctuates between good and evil.   Indecision will be as harmful as a bad choice.   Whether he advance or retire, let him remember that a chain of flowers is harder to break than one of iron.

Point VII.—*The Chariot of Osiris*

In the *Divine World :* The Sacred Septenary ; the dominion of Spirit over Matter.

In the *Intellectual World :* The despoiling of the older man, and the clothing of the new.

In the *Physical World :* Victory gained by intelligence ; the subjugation of the elements by the work of man.

In the *Horoscope :* The Empire of the World belongs to those who possess sovereignty of mind, that is to say, the light which explains the mysteries of life.   To overcome obstacles, to overcome enemies, and to fulfil one's vows, it is necessary to approach the future with a courage armed by the consciousness of right, but ever-mindful of one's duties.

Point VIII.—*The Balance and the Sword.*

In the *Divine World :* Absolute justice ; Divine protection, or chastisement.

In the *Intellectual World :* Attraction or repulsion ; things in equilibrium ; protection and conquest.

In the *Physical World :* the justice of men.

In the *Horoscope :* To conquer and to overcome obstacles is only one part of human duty ; to fully accomplish it one must establish an equilibrium between the forces that are put in play.   All action is followed by re-action ; in order to temper or nullify the shock of contrary forces the will must be prepared.   The future is wholly suspended between good and evil.   One should consult the spirit of truth and eternal justice, and beware of falling foul of the justice of man.

Point IX.—*The Veiled Lamp.*

In the *Divine World :* Absolute wisdom.

In the *Intellectual World :* Prudence, which directs the will.

In the *Physical World :* Circumspection, which directs action ; science, mystery.

In the *Horoscope :* Prudence is the armour of the sage.   Circumspection causes him to avoid the rocks and breakers of life, and to beware of treason.   A man should take it as his guide in all his acts, even in the merest trifles.   Nothing here below is unimportant : A pebble may alter the destinies of a man, or of an empire.   Let one remember that if speech be of silver, silence is of gold.

Point X.—*The Sphinx.*

In the *Divine World :* The principle which causes life.

In the *Intellectual World :* Authority, supremacy, genius.

In the *Physical World :* Good or bad fortune, rise or fall (according to the s gns and the planets which accompany or influence this point).

In the *Horoscope :* The Egyptian Sphinx is compounded of four natures ; it has a Human head, the body of a Bull, the claws of a Lion, and the wings of an Eagle.

The Human head, mark of intelligence, signifies that before entering into the struggle of life one should have acquired that knowledge which will illuminate the goal and the road.   The Bull's body signifies that, in face of the trials, the obstacles, and the dangers of life, one must be armed with a strong, patient, and persevering will in order to carve out the tenour of one's life.   The Lion's claws signify that to will with effect one must *dare* and make oneself room to the right or left, in front or behind, so as to be able to make freely that irresistible flight towards the heights of fortune which are indicated by the Eagle's wings.

If, therefore, a man know how to wish for that which is true ; if he only wish for that which is right ; if he dare that which he can attempt ; if he keep silence with regard to his plans ; if, through his perseverance, the morrow be only a continuation of the day before : *then* he will find one day under his hand the Key to *power*.

POINT XI.—*The Muzzled Lion.*

In the *Divine World :* The principle of every force.

In the *Intellectual World :* Moral force.

In the *Physical World :* Courage, contempt of danger, decision of character.

In the *Horoscope :* Forward with Faith ; obstacles are phantoms.   In order to be able one must believe oneself able.   In order to become strong one must silence repugnances of the mind and failings of the heart ; one must study *duty*, which is the ruler of *right*, and practise justice as if one loved it.

POINT XII.—*The Sacrifice.*

In the *Divine World :* The revealed law ; the divine punishment.

In the *Intellectual World :* The teaching of duty by repression ; madness ; culpable or criminal thoughts.

In the *Physical World :* Human punishment ; torture ; perpetual captivity ; violent death, either voluntary or sudden.

In the *Horoscope :* One should devote himself to others.   This is the Divine Law.   But one must not pay attention to the ingratitude of men. Let the subject hold himself at all times ready to render account of himself to the eternal, for death, sudden and violent, dogs his footsteps. But if the world slay him, let him not die without pardoning his enemies ; for he who does not pardon, throws himself into eternity armed with a dagger, and there is lost in the solitude and horror of self.

POINT XIII.—*The Reaping Skeleton.*

In the *Divine World :* Creation and transformation.

In the *Intellectual World :* The elevation of the mind.

In the *Physical World :* Death.

In the *Horoscope :* Let the subject raise his mind above earthly things, for the disappointment of his hopes gives menace of a shortened life ; his ambitions will be mowed down like the grass of the field.   The dissolution of the body will arrive prematurely, but let him not fear : Death is only the perpetual birth of humanity.   The voluntary enfranchisement of the instincts of matter, by the free adhesion of the mind to the laws of Universal Action, institutes in us the creation of " the New Man," and commences our Immortality.

Point XIV.—*The Two Urns.*

In the *Divine World* : Perpetual movement of Life.
In the *Intellectual World* : The combination of ideas, and the resultant solutions.
In the *Physical World* : The combination of elementary forces ; the relationship of the sexes.
In the *Horoscope* : Let the native consult his moral and physical powers, so not to give way before obstacles, but to overcome them little by little, as the drop of water wears away the stone. A well-thought-out course of action, calm, upright, and persevering, will give him the possession of that which he covets, and will raise him by degrees to those heights which he would attain.

Point XV.—*Typhon.*

In the *Divine World* : Predestination.
In the *Intellectual World* : Mystery ; the unknown.
In the *Physical World* : The unexpected ; fatality ; luxury.
In the *Horoscope* : The unexpected will nullify the prudence of the native ; the fatality will mar his future plans, if he restrain not his passions. He believes himself strong, and he is only a reed. The common oaks are not invulnerable ; how then can he expect to sustain the shock of unexpected catastrophes ?

Point XVI.—*The Blasted Tower.*

In the *Divine World* : Chastisement.
In the *Intellectual World* : The mind blasted by the Astral Fluid.
In the *Physical World* : Catastrophes ; loss of position ; ruin ; falls from high places.
In the *Horoscope* : The native goes to his destruction. It will be the fruit of his pride, of his imprudence, or voluntary misdeeds.

Point XVII.—*The Star of the Magicians.*

In the *Divine World* : The Three Virtues.
In the *Intellectual World* : Inward illumination.
In the *Physical World* : Hope ; the daughter of Faith, and the mother of Charity.
In the *Horoscope* : Let the native eschew passion and avoid error, so that he may study the mysteries of the Divine Science, and the key thereof will be given to him. Then, a ray of the Divine light will flash from the hidden sanctuary, it will dissipate the shadows from his future, and show him the path of happiness. Happen what may, let him not crush the flowers of Hope, and he will gather the fruits of faith.

Point XVIII.—*The Twilight.*

In the *Divine World* : The abysms of the infinite.
In the *Intellectual World* : Internal darkness.

In the *Physical World :* Deceptions, ambushes, snares, dangers from secret enemies.

In the *Horoscope :* Everything conspires against the native for his destruction, and he alone is ignorant of it. Hostile spirits, like the wolf, are laying snares for him ; servile spirits, denoted by the dog, hide their treason beneath a mask of flattery ; and idle spirits, denoted by the crab, will look upon his ruin without concern. Let him therefore be upon his guard, and retrace his steps, if there be yet time. Let him watch, listen, and act accordingly.

POINT XIX.—*The Resplendent Light.*

In the *Divine World :* The Supreme Heaven.

In the *Intellectual World :* The three joys of the hearth ; true happiness.

In the *Physical World :* Union, a happy marriage.

In the *Horoscope :* The native will be happy, and none will despoil him, if he knows how to guard it in the conjugal circle, and in the sanctuary of his heart.

POINT XX.—*The Awakening of the Dead.*

In the *Divine World :* the judgment of Conscience on the great day of the Spiritual Awakening.

In the *Intellectual World :* The revelation of genius.

In the *Physical World :* Unexpected elevation.

In the *Horoscope :* Let not the native fall asleep, either in idleness or forgetfulness ; he has a mission to accomplish, Providence will reveal it to him ; let him be ready when he hears the call.

POINT XXI.—*The Crown of the Magicians.*

This is the symbol of the highest elevation to which man can aspire. The supreme Talisman of fortune, this Crown denotes that every obstacle will disappear from the native's path, and that the ascension of his destiny has no limits save those of his will.

POINT XXII.—*The Blind Fool.*

This is the symbol of the man who has made himself the slave of material forces. His knapsack is full of his errors and mistakes. It denotes final catastrophes by foul enemies and unclean things.

In the *Horoscope :* Every kind of misfortune menaces the native. He must be wary in all things, for his safety can only be compassed by the compassion of Heaven.

FINIS